W9-AAT-115

WORLD CHAMPIONS 2019

WASHINGTON NATIONALS

General Manager Mike Rizzo and the Nationals celebrate after beating the Astros in Game 7 of the World Series. (Jonathan Newton/The Washington Post)

The Washington Post

Copyright © 2019 The Washington Post

BOOK STAFF
Matt Rennie, Deputy Sports Editor
Brian Gross, Deputy Design Director
Thomas Simonetti, Photo Editor
Brad Windsor, Copy Editor

Frederick J. Ryan Jr., Publisher and Chief Executive Officer
Martin Baron, Executive Editor
Cameron Barr, Managing Editor
Emilio Garcia-Ruiz, Managing Editor
Tracy Grant, Managing Editor
Matthew Vita, Sports Editor
Gregory Manifold, Design Director
MaryAnne Golon, Director of Photography
Dudley M. Brooks, Deputy Director of Photography
Robert Miller, Deputy Director of Photography

No part of this publication may be reproduced, stored
in a retrieval system or transmitted in any form by
any means, electronic, mechanical, photocopying
or otherwise, without prior written permission of the
publisher, Triumph Books LLC, 814 North Franklin Street;
Chicago, Illinois 60610.

This book is available in quantity at special discounts for
your group or organization.
For further information, contact:

Triumph Books LLC
814 North Franklin Street
Chicago, Illinois 60610
Phone: (312) 337-0747
www.triumphbooks.com

Printed in U.S.A.
ISBN: 978-1-62937-716-2

ON THE COVER
Anthony Rendon, Ryan Zimmerman and Asdrubal
Cabrera celebrate beating the Houston Astros.
(Front and back cover photos by Jonathan Newton)

Statistics: Sports-Reference.com

This is an unofficial publication. This book is in no way
affiliated with, licensed by or endorsed by Major League
Baseball or the Washington Nationals.

It's a red October at Nationals Park for the
first World Series game in D.C. since 1933.
(Toni L. Sandys/The Washington Post)

INTRODUCTION

Indomitable team, improbable run won't be forgotten

By Thomas Boswell

From left, Juan Soto, Adam Eaton and Victor Robles celebrate winning Game 2 of the World Series between the Nationals and Astros. (Jonathan Newton / The Washington Post)

After the final strike of the 2019 World Series settled in catcher Yan Gomes's glove and Washington was driven shark-raving mad, the thoughts and passions of Nationals fans flew in countless directions.

When the jubilant "Stay in the Fight" Nats dashed to the pitcher's mound to rejoice in D.C.'s first major league title in 95 years, emotions flooded through a fan base so diverse that it stretches from 94-year-old team owner Ted Lerner, who went to the 1937 All-Star Game at Griffith Stadium, to the newest "May I jump on this bandwagon, please" fans who just discovered how thrilling and inspiring baseball can be, especially when their Nats pull off Game 6 and 7 victories on the road.

Seldom has there been such a perfect marriage of a team with players of every imaginable background and a kaleidoscopic fan base.

These world champion Nats are jokingly called the Internationals because they come from almost every nationality and background found in baseball as well as every rung in the status structure of the game. They are a team of superstars, such as pitchers Max Scherzer, Stephen Strasburg and Patrick Corbin, whose combined contracts are worth more than a half-billion dollars, and heart-of-the-order hitters Anthony Rendon and Juan Soto.

But it is also a team of proud, defiant older players, the kind now cast aside by much of baseball. Howie Kendrick, the MVP of the National League Championship Series, is 36, and so is catcher Kurt Suzuki, whose home run ignited the Nats' vital victory in Game 2 of the World Series. The onetime face of the franchise, Ryan Zimmerman, missed months because of a heel injury he has battled for years — with the heel usually winning. But in the postseason, he seemed young and powerful again.

With 18 players in the World Series past 30, the oldest team in baseball called itself Los Viejos — the old-timers.

The beloved symbol of the team, outfielder Gerardo Parra, barely plays, and when he does, he comes to the plate to a walk-up song, "Baby Shark," that is a silly, infectious ditty beloved by toddlers. Yet the entire Nationals Park crowd stands to honor him with its "chomps." This is a team where the last shall be first, where a castoff such as Parra can find a home and where no one dares act like a star.

Those who are filled with unexpected joy now — those who never dreamed of this May 23, when the Nats were 19-31 and baseball's No. 1 embarrassment of the season — are as different as the men they cheer.

The roars, which will ring in our ears all winter and reverberate in our memories for a lifetime, may come from someone such as me, who became a Washington baseball fan before the original Senators skipped town after the 1960 season to become the Minnesota Twins.

Maybe that fan yelling in joy at the TV set caught the baseball bug in the days of the expansion Senators, with slugger Frank Howard, before that team also left D.C. after the 1971 season to become the Texas Rangers.

Perhaps, like my son, who grew up during D.C.'s 33 years without a team, you yelled for the Nats and grinned, even though you grew up trekking to Memorial Stadium, then Camden Yards, with Dad to pull for Washington's make-do surrogate team, the Baltimore Orioles.

Best of all, at least for the Nationals of the future, tons of those yells, much of the roaring at watch parties, in bars and restaurants and in homes all over the DMV, came from the fans of the new Nationals — nee Montreal Expos — who came to D.C. in 2005.

For now, for this moment of generational arm-linking, it is fitting to mention Walter Johnson, who won Game 7 of the 1924 World Series in relief, though hardly a living soul who saw it is still around.

For now, it is fine and dandy to watch those amazing old newsreels of 40,000 fans at Griffith Stadium dashing onto the diamond after Muddy Ruel stomped on home plate to claim that old title, until they covered every yard of the playing surface.

But the importance of the Nats' 2019 World Series triumph is all about the future. Washington is now a normal baseball city, with more than ample reason to hold its head high and wear its gear proudly.

With respect, we can lay to rest all the defeats, disappointments, deferrals of joy and disrespect at the hands of Major League Baseball, which defined and distorted the first 118 years of the relationship between D.C. and the professional game.

This is a fresh start — and the best sort — that was earned with a reasonable amount of dues-paying but not enough misery to mar the future. The Nats' first-round playoff exits in 2012, 2014, 2016 and 2017 — three of them featuring excruciating Game 5 losses — now feel like a painful initiation. But with a World Series flag to raise at Nats Park next spring, those years feel like prologue, not abuse.

Other teams have a "Nation," a common heritage. Perhaps it is a Billy Goat or Bambino Curse that finally has been overcome.

Maybe it is a legacy of Pinstripe Pride, Dodger Blue or the Cardinal Way that gets handed down through generations. Maybe it is Moneyball Make-Do savvy.

Until now, the Nationals just had a diaspora, including countless "transients" who lived here — some staying, some going and taking D.C. baseball loyalties with them. Now, a unifying tradition can start to lock itself in place around a team that has dispelled its postseason ghosts, built the second-best regular season record in baseball over the past eight years and secured the one flag that validates its team-building philosophies.

At the age of 72, as a lifelong Washingtonian and a baseball-loving sportswriter at The Washington Post for the past 50 years, I have a history and emotions that either mirror, or intersect with, those of many Nationals followers. Also, as someone who has covered every World Series game since 1975, I share some of their delighted confusion. Even for those of us who saw the whole surge that built over the Nats' final 112 regular season games — a 74-38 record with a huge positive run differential that essentially matched any team in the sport — the whole month of October still has a marvelous aura of "How the hell did that happen?" Seldom has a team overcome as much or won more convincingly against such seemingly insurmountable postseason odds as these Nationals.

Somewhere, as autumn turns toward winter, Milwaukee fans will remember a line-drive single to right field by 20-year-old superstar Soto that drove in two runs to tie the wild-card game, then took a bad hop past a Brewers outfielder to allow the game-winner to score too.

In Los Angeles — where winter never visits but neither has a World Series crown in the past 31 years — the Dodgers will remember back-to-back home runs by Rendon and Soto off the immortal but October-cursed Clayton Kershaw to tie Game 5 of the NL Division Series. Perhaps the sunsets at Malibu will help them forget that Manager Dave Roberts left in average reliever Joe Kelly to pitch the 10th inning, then left him there until the bases were loaded, then unloaded, by Kendrick's grand slam.

In a tie for Most Bewildered Big Leaguers will be every member of the Central Division champion St. Louis Cardinals and the 107-win Houston Astros. They were told that they would play a Washington team that won a respectable but hardly intimidating 93 games in the regular season and … and the fourth-worst bullpen in the past 50 years.

In other words, a team to beat.

Instead, the Cardinals did not win a game in the NLCS. They barely scored a run. And if all their hits combined in those four winless games were feathers, there would not be enough of them to keep one poor cardinal warm this winter.

The proud-to-the-point-of-vanity Astros will be the most numbed of all.

Just as they, and almost every sports gambler, believed that American League Cy Young Award candidates Gerrit Cole (326 strikeouts) and Justin Verlander (300) would give the Astros a quick two-game lead, the Nationals countered Houston's kings with their own mound aces. Scherzer and Strasburg won both pitching showdowns, allowing just two runs each to the powerhouse Houston attack, and got the wins.

Now, Nats fans will have the long, glorious offseason to rewind and replay, to relish their delighted disbelief, as they meditate on Baby Sharks and dugout dance lines, on group hugs eliciting sheepish grins and on Manager Dave Martinez's successful bullpen machinations throughout October.

Yes, the same Martinez who I wrote should be fired in May. And, yes, the same Nationals who many pundits coast-to-coast said had no hope at 19-31 and simply should sell off their marketable stars, such as Rendon and Scherzer, to rebuild for the future.

As is the way with long-awaited World Series triumphs many thought they would never see, there is a place for personal digression, a.k.a. self-indulgence. I'll keep it short, promise.

On an October afternoon in 1956, I walked home from Peabody Elementary School to our house on Lexington Place NE on Capitol Hill in Washington, D.C. When I got to the door, I heard screaming and yelling inside. Inside, I found my mom and my godfather, who had played minor league baseball for the Philadelphia A's, jumping up and down in front of our black-and-white television.

"Don Larsen just pitched a perfect game in the World Series," my mother announced. Because not everyone had a TV in those days, believe it or not, my godfather, who lived down the street, had come over to watch. That is when, at age 8, I discovered that baseball drove people crazy in a wonderful, transformative way — even my mother, whom I'd never seen so excited.

The next day, Washington Post sports columnist Shirley Povich wrote his most famous newspaper lede: "The million-to-one shot came in. Hell froze over. A month of Sundays hit the calendar. Don Larsen today pitched a no-hit, no-run, no-man-reach-first game in a World Series."

I was already a fan, but from roughly that point, I became a "baseball fanatic" — the technical term for someone who is made unreasonably and persistently happy by baseball for the rest of his or her life, through bad times and good. My team: the Senators, also called the Nationals, who were always awful and had won the World Series only once since they came into existence in 1901.

For the next 56 years, as I remained a fan, Washington had one winning team: in 1969, the year I became a young coffee-fetcher in the Post sports department. But even that team finished in "the second division," the bottom half of the American League.

Povich, my colleague, and later friend for 29 years, was the greatest proponent and defender of D.C. baseball in the town's history. But as irony would have it, he wasted his famous lede on an utterly unworthy subject — a mere perfect game in the World Series by yet another iteration of the dynastic Yanks he always respected but detested.

When Shirley died, at age 92, in 1998, he would still have needed to live another 21 years to see his city have a parade for a World Series winner. So, I suppose, I'll be his posthumous editor and blue-pencil his Larsen lede into a form I bet he'd have loved: "The million-to-one shot came in. Hell froze over. A month of Sundays hit the calendar. The Washington Nationals, a team given a one-tenth-of-a-percent chance to win the pennant in late May, won the championship of baseball just five months later in a feat that makes a perfect game in the World Series seem palely prosaic in comparison."

If Shirley's ghost could leap into Strasburg's arms, it would.

While Larsen's perfect game was the deed of a day, the Nationals' accomplishment will be a joy and an inspiration for decades, if not generations. In a time when Washington symbolized the antithesis of fundamental American values to millions, the diverse, group-hugging, dugout-dancing Nationals represented the best in fundamental baseball values to everyone.

The Nats were a mutually supportive, joyous, multicultural steamroller that went beyond tolerance to unconditional love of its weakest members: its mind-bending bullpen. Yes, I saved the bullpen.

Both anecdotally and statistically, baseball doctrine tells us that nothing undermines a team, destroys its morale and turns it against itself internally as much as a blown save that leads to defeat in the late innings after the entire team has spent hours building a lead.

Yet for an entire season, right into the playoffs and through the World Series, the star-filled Nationals' internal stance toward its weak links was a sincere: "Thanks for your best effort. Come back tomorrow, smiling, and we'll try to go 1-0."

From General Manager Mike Rizzo, the brilliant team architect, to Martinez, the manager he stood behind, through all the team's biggest names, the 2019 Nats stood for the oldest, corniest and best sports values: Together, they were teamwork, modesty, fun, resilience, dancing and hugging.

They were Adam Eaton and Kendrick sitting together in the dugout, after either one of them hit a home run, acting like they were driving racecars, shifting gears and making roaring noises while doing it.

Almost unique in baseball, they were an organization that combined new analytics insights with old scouting wisdom. Two of the sets of eyes on whom Rizzo depended were former GM and manager Jack McKeon and his own father, Phil — ages 88 and 89. Rizzo said he was inspired "by their youthful enthusiasm."

The Nats were about blending cultures into brotherhood. Living one day, even one pitch at a time, because your situation is too precarious to handle a larger load. They were about a stoic such as Strasburg learning to enjoy himself, his gifts and his teammates.

The Nats were also about self-criticism and apologies to others. Fans, and media, learned to say "I'm sorry" to Martinez as they realize that he knows how to manage people and set a tone of relaxed enjoyment in an ultra-stressful job. Camel jokes died a glorious death.

As to whether Martinez could manage a bullpen, he used all his Big Three aces in crucial high-leverage spots throughout October.

All three star pitchers battled to see who could raise his hand faster to volunteer. Without that strategy, and the manager's real-time handling of it, there would be no World Series winner in Washington now.

Say it again, and again: "World Series winner" and "Washington."

Say it all winter. Some of you believe that these words truly can fit together, belong together, even after 95 years. You feel it, believe it and have internalized it permanently.

The rest of us, smiling all the way, will get there. Just give us time.

The Nationals erupt in joy after winning Game 7 to secure the franchise's first championship. (Jonathan Newton/The Washington Post)

World class

Nationals starting pitcher Max Scherzer raises the Commissioner's Trophy.
(Jonathan Newton/The Washington Post)

By Dave Sheinin

Suddenly, it was all over, and the blue-jerseyed visitors were spilling and screaming out of every corner of Minute Maid Park — from their dugout along the third base line, the bullpen in left field, the expanse of outfield, all four corners of the diamond — and converging upon the joyous pile of humanity forming near the center. Once the Washington Nationals had no more giant mountains to climb, they took the small dirt hill of the pitcher's mound, and they hugged and bounced.

With one more comeback win, at the end of a comeback season for the ages, the Nationals were World Series champions. A 6-2 victory over the Houston Astros in Game 7 on Wednesday night sealed it, delivering the first major league title for the nation's capital since Walter Johnson's Senators won their only one in 1924.

Having existed for the better part of five months as a decided underdog — their odds of winning the World Series back on May 24, when they were 19-31, were 1.5 percent — the Nationals had come to live for the daily fight for their lives. And now, the fight was over.

Seventh-inning home runs by Anthony Rendon and Howie Kendrick, the former an MVP-caliber third baseman possibly playing his last game in a Nationals uniform, the latter a 36-year-old veteran in the deepest autumn of his career, turned a slim deficit into a slim lead for the Nationals. A tacked-on run in the eighth and two more in the ninth provided breathing room.

The final out, delivered by reliever Daniel Hudson, settled into catcher Yan Gomes's glove at 10:50 p.m. Central time, touching off the mad dash to the center of the diamond. A hushed crowd of 43,326 watched the visitors celebrate as the Astros slouched off the field.

And so ended the longest season in Washington baseball history — one that began on a chilly Thursday in late March, cratered in late May, caught fire in the summer months, tested hearts in September and careened through October like a wobble-wheeled wagon set free at the top of a steep hill. This Nationals season was a wild, screaming, impossibly long ride, one that carried them all the way to the doorstep of November.

Take a step back and consider what these Nationals accomplished: They notched all four of their wins in this series on the road, in the building where the Astros had the majors' best home record in 2019, and became the first team since the 2016 Chicago Cubs to take the World Series by winning Games 6 and 7 on the road. They outhit an Astros offense that ranked among the most potent in history. They hung losses on the Astros' twin aces — Gerrit Cole in Game 1, Justin Verlander in Games 2 and 6 — and outlasted yet another Houston ace, Zack Greinke, on Wednesday night.

"To win four games on the road in the World Series," said first baseman Ryan Zimmerman, the longest-tenured National, "it's almost fitting for us."

On a makeshift stage moments after the final out, pitcher Stephen Strasburg, the overpowering victor of Games 2 and 6, was presented with the Series' MVP trophy. The Lerner family, which has owned the team since 2006, stood alongside General Manager Mike Rizzo and Manager Davey Martinez and lifted the Commissioner's Trophy. Players hugged and waved to their families below. Pitcher Max Scherzer stood off to the side and cried openly.

"I'm speechless," principal owner Mark Lerner said. "I've dreamed of this my entire life."

There had never been an October like this in the nation's capital, one so full of baseball and life. The last time a Washington team played in the World Series, the original Senators in 1933, it ended Oct. 7. But in the current, expanded playoff format, with 10 teams and four rounds, this October stretched on for week upon glorious week — an exhilarating ride that took them from Nationals Park on the first night of the month to Houston's Minute Maid Park the night before Halloween.

Those two bookend games, the win-or-go-home wild-card game that launched the Nationals' October and the Game 7 start Wednesday night that ended it, had one thing in common: They were both started by Scherzer.

Three nights earlier, the Nationals' veteran ace could barely get himself out of bed and couldn't raise his pitching arm, because of a severe bout of neck spasms that would force the team to scratch him from his Game 5 start at Nationals Park on Sunday night. Getting him ready to pitch Wednesday night required a cortisone shot, ample rest and perhaps divine intervention.

Getting him past the Astros' lineup, the best in baseball this season, would not be as easy.

Scherzer lived in near-constant danger throughout his five innings of work, allowing only a pair of runs but pitching with traffic on the base paths throughout. One of the great strikeout pitchers of his era, he didn't record his first in Game 7 until his 17th batter of the night. It was Scherzer's great fortune that the vast majority of the Astros' line drives and deep smashes landed in the gloves of his teammates.

That Martinez had failed to get a reliever warmed up as a clearly diminished Scherzer was allowing the Astros' second run to score in the fifth seemed to be either an egregious mistake or a staggering show of faith in his ace. By the time the fifth ended, the Astros led 2-0 but already had stranded nine base runners.

In other words, after a month of exquisite play and narrow escapes, Game 7 had carried the Nationals to a familiar place. They had spent so much of the past five months playing from behind — from the long slog of digging out of May's 19-31 hole to the win-or-go-home games of early and mid-October — that it almost brought a perverse sense of comfort. They were at their best, they liked to say, when their backs were to the wall.

Wednesday night marked their fifth elimination game of the month, where a loss would end the season, following one at Nationals Park in the wild-card game, two against the Los Angeles Dodgers in the division series and Tuesday night's Game 6 win over the Astros. They had trailed in all of them, storming back each time to win. Their reputation as the sport's ultimate fighters was well earned.

The seventh inning homers by Rendon and Kendrick — the former a no-doubt blast into the stands in left, the latter a bending, twisting, opposite field drive that clanged off the right field foul pole — were merely confirmation. Suddenly, the Nationals' 2-0 deficit was a 3-2 lead, and they were nine outs from winning the World Series.

By Wednesday night, the Nationals were running on a cocktail of thin fumes, painkillers, Red Bulls and dwindling supplies of adrenaline. Each player was reduced to his component parts and what each had left — how many pitches, how many innings, how many competitive at-bats.

After all the speculation about how the Nationals might piece together the necessary 27 outs for victory, it was as tidy an affair as they could have dreamed. Scherzer went five, giving way to left-hander Patrick Corbin, their Game 4 starter, now pitching on short rest, who handled the next three without incident. And finally, Hudson entered for the ninth and set down the Astros.

"I kept counting down the outs in my head," said shortstop Trea Turner. "Nine more outs. Eight …"

Throughout this month, the Nationals left their fans a trove of memory-book moments: Soto's eighth-inning, three-run single off Milwaukee Brewers bullpen ace Josh Hader to lift the Nationals to victory in the wild-card game, the back-to-back homers from Rendon and Soto off Los Angeles Dodgers ace Clayton Kershaw in the eighth inning to tie Game 5 of the division series and Howie Kendrick's grand slam two innings later off Joe Kelly to push the Nationals ahead.

The World Series alone featured two excellent starts from Strasburg, three homers from Soto and a heroic effort by Scherzer just to get himself to the mound for Game 7.

The Astros may have been baseball's best team in the regular season — a 107-win juggernaut out of the top-heavy American League, with an offense that ranks among the best in history and a rotation headed by a trio of aces — but they were outplayed across seven games by the Nationals, humble wild card winners out of the National League.

To the very end, the Nationals played with a joy and camaraderie that are impossible to fake. They were an Internet meme come to life, with their dugout dance parties, "Baby Shark" singalongs, pink sunglasses, Soto Shuffles, champagne-soaked renditions of Latin pop hit "Calma" and ubiquitous catchphrase: "Stay in the Fight."

The fight lasted as long as it possibly could, through the final date on the baseball calendar. Washington had waited 95 years for another World Series champion. But the wait is over. The next time anyone sees this team, it will be at the championship parade down Constitution Avenue on Saturday.

Nationals hold on to steal first game

Juan Soto's three hits included a game-tying solo home run in the fourth inning.
(Jonathan Newton / The Washington Post)

By Jesse Dougherty

T he calculations began days ago, inside Dave Martinez's crowded brain, on any scraps of paper the Washington Nationals manager could find, but now they were kicked straight into overdrive.

It was, after all, Game 1 of the World Series. There was very little room for error. There was just a three-run lead to protect, and Max Scherzer running on fumes by the fifth inning, and then only the biggest decisions Martinez has ever made on a baseball field. And after he did, carefully stacking one move on top of another, the Nationals had pushed ahead of the Houston Astros for a 5-4 win at Minute Maid Park on Tuesday night.

They did it by handing Astros starter Gerrit Cole his first loss in five months. They did it, really, despite ditching their weeks-long strategy of going all in and leaving the consequences for later. Scherzer exited after throwing 112 pitches in five innings. That led Martinez to Patrick Corbin, one of his four starters, for three outs in relief. But next came Tanner Rainey, in the biggest spot of his young career, and he yielded a solo homer to George Springer before issuing back-to-back walks.

Daniel Hudson then stranded the bases that were loaded in the seventh, gave up a run in the eighth and handed the mess to Sean Doolittle. But Doolittle recorded a four-out save to sidestep a collapse. Juan Soto's three-hit, three-RBI effort was not wasted. The bullpen tested fate, and for the first time in 86 years, a Washington baseball team took a World Series game.

"It's a huge win for us no matter who we were facing," Corbin said. "But [Cole] has been one of their guys all year, and they have a great pitcher going tomorrow. All these games seem like they are going to be like this. It's two good teams fighting."

In the days between the National League Championship Series and World Series — Washington had six of them — Martinez often plotted Game 1 in his head. The Nationals had a long layoff after sweeping the St. Louis Cardinals in the NLCS. That gave Martinez time to think, then think some more, about who could account for 27 outs against the Astros' dynamic lineup. It would begin with Scherzer, that was sure, but there was intricate planning beyond that. Martinez had spent all postseason avoiding his middle relievers, Rainey included, and that was the ideal approach against the Astros.

Martinez didn't say that when asked how he pictured the beginning of the series. He didn't have to.

"I imagined it could be really good," Martinez said with a laugh Tuesday afternoon. "What do you want me to imagine?"

By 7:10 p.m. in Houston, when Cole fired a first-pitch ball to Trea Turner, imagination turned into reality. That went for Martinez, who had been this far as a bench coach in 2008 and again eight years later, yet never as a manager. That went for his players, most of whom hadn't been this deep into October, who had only dreamed about it in backyards and on boring afternoons. And that went for Washington, and the fans who lost baseball for decades, and a city that hadn't had a World Series team since 1933.

They arrived here Tuesday, all together, all washing past heartache with newfound hope. But the Astros had sprinted through the regular season and finished with a major league-best 107 wins. They were the heavy favorites in this series, according to Las Vegas, and are looking for their second title in the past three falls. They also had not lost a game started by Cole since July 12.

That trend seemed likely to continue once Scherzer allowed two runs in the first. Cole, on the other hand, had allowed just one earned run in $22^2/_3$ innings so far this postseason. But no one told that to Washington.

Nationals 5, Astros 4

WASHINGTON	AB	R	H	BI	BB	SO	AVG
Turner ss	4	0	1	0	0	1	.283
Eaton rf	4	0	2	1	0	0	.225
Rendon 3b	4	1	0	0	0	1	.333
Soto lf	4	1	3	3	0	1	.286
Kendrick dh	4	0	0	0	0	0	.262
Cabrera 2b	4	0	1	0	0	2	.154
Zimmerman 1b	4	1	1	1	0	1	.286
Suzuki c	3	1	0	0	1	1	.043
Robles cf	4	1	1	0	0	1	.300
TOTALS	**35**	**5**	**9**	**5**	**1**	**8**	**—**

HOUSTON	AB	R	H	BI	BB	SO	AVG
Springer cf	3	2	2	2	2	1	.184
Altuve 2b	5	1	1	0	0	1	.333
Brantley lf-rf	4	0	1	0	1	1	.261
Bregman 3b	4	0	0	0	1	3	.231
Gurriel 1b	5	0	2	2	0	1	.229
Correa ss	5	0	1	0	0	3	.174
Alvarez dh	3	0	2	0	1	1	.205
Maldonado c	3	0	0	0	0	1	.250
Tucker ph	1	1	1	0	0	0	.222
Chirinos c	0	0	0	0	0	0	.091
Reddick rf	2	0	0	0	0	0	.125
Diaz ph-lf	2	0	0	0	0	0	.000
TOTALS	**37**	**4**	**10**	**4**	**5**	**12**	**—**

WASHINGTON	010	130	000	—	5	9	0
HOUSTON	200	000	110	—	4	10	0

LOB: Washington 4, Houston 11. **2B:** Soto (2), Gurriel (2), Springer (1). **HR:** Zimmerman (2), off Cole; Soto (3), off Cole; Springer (3), off Rainey. **RBI:** Zimmerman (6), Soto 3 (10), Eaton (5), Gurriel 2 (10), Springer 2 (6). **SB:** Turner (1), Altuve (2), Soto (1). **DP:** Houston 1 (Altuve, Correa, Gurriel).

WASHINGTON	IP	H	R	ER	BB	SO	NP	ERA
Scherzer	5	5	2	2	3	7	112	2.16
Corbin	1	1	0	0	0	2	21	6.91
Rainey	0.1	1	1	1	2	1	19	6.23
Hudson	1.1	3	1	1	0	1	21	1.29
Doolittle	1.1	0	0	0	0	1	13	2.08

HOUSTON	IP	H	R	ER	BB	SO	NP	ERA
Cole	7	8	5	5	1	6	104	1.82
Harris	1	1	0	0	0	1	18	0.00
Smith	1	0	0	0	1	6	1.42

WP: Scherzer, (3-0); **LP:** Cole, (3-1); **S:** Doolittle, (2). **Inherited runners-scored:** Hudson 2-0, Doolittle 1-0. **WP:** Scherzer. **T:** 3:43. **A:** 43,339 (41,168).

Ryan Zimmerman gets a hug from Gerardo Parra after his homer gave the Nationals their first run. (John McDonnell/The Washington Post)

Ryan Zimmerman revved the Nationals with a solo shot off Cole in the second. He was the first pick in club history, way back in the spring of 2005, and now scored its first ever World Series run. Zimmerman later described himself as "kind of floating around the bases." He'd put a crack, however slight, in Cole's unshakable dominance.

Then, two frames later, Soto became just the fourth player to hit a World Series homer before his 21st birthday, joining Andruw Jones, Miguel Cabrera and Mickey Mantle on that list. Soto was comfortable with Cole's velocity because of his experience facing the righty at the teams' shared spring training facility in West Palm Beach, Fla. The blast came on almost the same pitch Soto struck out on in the first, a high-and-away fastball, and he parked it on the steel tracks well beyond the left field wall. A makeshift train up there moves whenever the Astros score. It's not used to having baseballs fly into its path.

"It starts off with breaking the ice," General Manager Mike Rizzo said of beating Cole. "And Zim hit a really good pitch really far and really hard. That got us going. That kind of broke the ice."

The Nationals stretched out a lead in the fifth, first on Adam Eaton's RBI single, then when Soto ripped a two-run double off the left field wall. Soto looked into the dugout before tangling his fists in celebration. And the immediate question inside it, where Martinez sat among his coaches, was who could get the final 15 outs?

Scherzer handled the first three. Corbin needed 21 pitches to get through a scoreless sixth. Martinez could have pushed him and taxed his arm on what was a typical throw day, but one inning was always the plan with a possible Game 3 start in mind. Then Rainey yielded that homer to Springer, recorded just one out and, for an encore, walked two before Martinez hooked him. Then Hudson avoided further damage in that inning, covering for Rainey, before yielding an RBI double to Springer in the eighth.

That pulled Houston to within a run. That made it easy to recall every single time the Nationals' bullpen faltered this season. Hudson recovered for one more out, a liner that found Eaton's mitt, and that's when Martinez made one last walk to the mound. In came Doolittle, who lost the closer role in August, who needed two weeks for his arm and right knee to heal, and whose whole career had been building to a moment such as this. So he retired all four batters he faced and, with that, gave Washington control of the World Series.

Imagine that.

Nats take command of series with rout

Adam Eaton dances in the dugout after smacking a two-run homer in the eighth inning. (Toni L. Sandys/ The Washington Post)

By Jesse Dougherty

By the end of the seventh inning Wednesday night, by the time they had batted around, bullied the Houston Astros and brought themselves within two wins of a title — with five chances to get them — the Washington Nationals could take just a second to look around and breathe.

They were the enemies in a stadium that was slowly emptying out. Enemies with big grins and even bigger reasons to bet on themselves. That's what happens when you beat the home team, 12-3, in Game 2 of the World Series. That's what happens when you carry a 2-0 lead onto a plane back to Washington. That's what happens when you stage a six-run seventh inning that starts against star pitcher Justin Verlander and ends with you capitalizing on every last mistake.

That's what the Nationals did at Minute Maid Park. They dismembered the Astros, and in swift fashion, after Stephen Strasburg kept them floating in a tight game. He gave up two runs in six innings of taxing work. He was rewarded once the bats erupted in the seventh. The rally began when Kurt Suzuki rocketed a Verlander fastball out to left. It only finished when the Nationals had marched into Houston and left little doubt.

Fifty-five teams have taken a 2-0 advantage in the World Series. Forty-four have won it all.

"You know what, I wish I was a betting man," Manager Dave Martinez said of his club having less than a 1 percent chance to make it here in mid-May. "But I'm not. I don't really believe in that stuff."

Verlander was first tasked with slowing a team that has now won eight games in a row and 18 of its past 20 going back to Sept. 23. But he couldn't, at least at the start and finish, beginning when Anthony Rendon smacked a two-run double in the first. The fans went quiet, and their orange flags didn't wave, yet it didn't take long for the building to fill with noise. Washington's early 2-0 lead lasted until Alex Bregman hit a towering two-run shot off Strasburg in the bottom of the inning.

He rocked a middle-in change-up, but Strasburg was quick to find a rhythm. Verlander was, too. Strasburg eventually fought through six innings on 114 pitches. He stranded two runners before he exited, giving the Nationals a chance and gutting a spurt of Verlander's dominance with more of his own. Strasburg capped the outing by getting Kyle Tucker to wave at a full-count curveball. He jogged off the field once he did, leaving nothing behind, and locked hands with first base coach Tim Bogar in a swinging high-five.

Strasburg typically ducks into the tunnel once he exits. He finds a quiet space. He waits for the pitching coach to tell him he is done. But now Strasburg knew the job was finished. So he walked through a line of teammates, repeated two words — "Come on! Come on!" — then left them to celebrate when Suzuki started the next half-inning with a boom.

"Those guys are going out there and giving us literally everything they have every single pitch," right fielder Adam Eaton said of the Nationals' rotation, "and pitching through some different situations and putting our offense in a good situation. And that's all we can ask."

The Nationals put together intricate scouting reports for their hitters to review each series. It's a joint job for the analytics and video staffs. But a member of the organization once joked that Suzuki's packet is always thinner than the rest. He just looks for the first fastball he sees and tries to pull it as hard as he can. And that's what he did against Verlander in the seventh, smashing high heat, driving it off the Lexus sign behind the left field seats and down into the stands.

Nationals 12, Astros 3

WASHINGTON	AB	R	H	BI	BB	SO	AVG
Turner ss	4	2	1	0	2	2	.250
Eaton rf	4	2	2	2	0	0	.500
Parra ph-rf	1	0	0	0	0	0	.000
Rendon 3b	4	0	1	2	1	1	.125
Soto lf	3	2	1	0	2	1	.571
Kendrick dh	5	1	2	1	0	0	.222
Cabrera 2b	5	1	2	3	0	3	.333
Zimmerman 1b	5	0	2	1	0	1	.333
Suzuki c	5	1	2	1	0	0	.250
Robles cf	3	2	0	0	1	2	.143
Taylor cf	1	1	1	1	0	0	1.00
TOTALS	40	12	14	11	6	10	—

HOUSTON	AB	R	H	BI	BB	SO	AVG
Springer cf-rf	5	0	0	0	0	1	.250
Altuve 2b	5	0	3	0	0	0	.400
Brantley lf	4	1	2	0	0	0	.375
Marisnick cf	1	0	0	0	0	0	.000
Bregman 3b	4	1	1	2	0	0	.125
Gurriel 1b	4	0	1	0	0	1	.333
Alvarez dh	3	0	1	0	1	1	.500
Correa ss	4	0	0	0	0	1	.111
Chirinos c	2	0	0	0	0	2	.000
Tucker ph	1	0	0	0	0	1	.500
Maldonado c	1	1	1	1	0	0	.250
Reddick rf-lf	3	0	0	0	1	1	.000
TOTALS	37	3	9	3	2	8	—

WASHINGTON	200	000	631	—	12 14 2
HOUSTON	200	000	001	—	3 9 1

E: Turner (1), Rendon (1), Bregman (1). **LOB:** Washington 8, Houston 9. **2B:** Rendon (1), Soto (2), Altuve (1), Gurriel (2). **HR:** Suzuki (1), off Verlander; Eaton (1), off James; Taylor (1), off Devenski; Bregman (1), off Strasburg; Maldonado (1), off Guerra. **RBI:** Rendon 2 (2), Suzuki (1), Kendrick (1), Cabrera 3 (3), Zimmerman (2), Eaton 2 (3), Taylor (1), Bregman 2 (2), Maldonado (1). **CS:** Altuve (1). **S:** Eaton. **DP:** Houston 1 (Correa, Gurriel).

WASHINGTON	IP	H	R	ER	BB	SO	NP	ERA
Strasburg	6	7	2	2	1	7	114	3.00
Rodney	1	0	0	0	1	0	21	0.00
Rainey	1	0	0	0	0	1	12	6.75
Guerra	1	2	1	1	0	0	15	9.00

HOUSTON	IP	H	R	ER	BB	SO	NP	ERA
Verlander	6	7	4	4	3	6	107	6.00
Pressly	2	3	4	3	2	0	22	40.5
James	1	2	3	1	1	3	27	9.00
Rondon	1	1	0	0	0	0	8	0.00
Devenski	1	1	1	1	0	1	15	9.00

WP: Strasburg (1-0); **LP:** Verlander (0-1). **Inherited runners-scored:** Pressly 1-1, James 1-0, Rondon 2-1. **IBB:** off Strasburg (Alvarez), off Pressly (Soto). **WP:** Pressly. **PB:** Maldonado (0). **T:** 4:01. **A:** 43,357 (41,168).

Justin Verlander, falling while trying to field a ball, allowed four runs. (Jonathan Newton / The Washington Post)

Verlander was hooked for reliever Ryan Pressly after he walked Victor Robles with no outs. The floodgates soon opened when Turner walked, and with two outs, the Astros issued their first intentional pass of the entire season. It put Juan Soto on first to load the bases. Houston paid for it once Bregman bobbled a Kendrick grounder, allowing a run and the rally to continue, before Asdrúbal Cabrera drove in two with a single. Then Bregman erred again by throwing a ball high and wide of first to allow two more Nationals to score. Big pockets of the crowd headed for the exits. And the ballpark went silent again.

"We're getting contributions from guys up and down the roster," closer Sean Doolittle said. "Our stars are playing like stars, but we're getting contributions from guys one through nine in the order."

So when Martinez reflected on the game, and he had some time to do so, it was hard to pick the hero. There was Rendon lifting that two-run double in the first. There was Strasburg keeping the Astros in check for six innings. There was Suzuki's home run, there was Cabrera pitching in, and there were all the tiny contributions that, when glued together, formed a winning whole. The challenge was that Martinez had to decide.

Before this season, his second on the job, an idea popped into Martinez's head. The manager wanted to save a game ball from every one of Washington's wins. He wanted to put them on a wall outside his office at Nationals Park, set in chronological order, stacked on shelves that grew as the season moved along. Each is signed by the player who led the Nationals to victory. When Martinez can't pick one, when the effort feels bigger, he has two players scratch their signatures onto the worn leather. Some even have three names. Then Martinez finishes the process by writing the date on a plastic case and putting it in its spot for good.

When the Nationals left for Houston on Monday, there were 101 game balls stretching from March 31 to Oct. 15. They formed a mural of team success. Players often stand in the hallway to look, remembering the most random days of an eight-month sprint, counting how many they have accounted for. Now Martinez will leave here with a fresh pair to shelve: There is Soto's ball after he collected three hits and three RBI in Game 1. There will be another signed by Strasburg from Wednesday.

And the Nationals need just two more.

Nats waste opportunities, squander shot at 3-0 lead

By Jesse Dougherty

Trea Turner peeled himself off the dirt, his head shaking, his knees a bit weak, before waving at strike three in a sixth inning that showed all the Washington Nationals didn't do Friday night. Then Adam Eaton thought he had struck out right after, by the inches of a check swing, until it was ruled he didn't go. Two Nationals were on base. Eaton stood, for a short moment, as the tying run.

But the right fielder bounced a ball to first, diminishing the Nationals' final threat and directing attention to what's now at hand in a tightened World Series. The Houston Astros beat the Nationals, 4-1, in Game 3 on Friday night. It pulled the series to 2-1, with the Nationals still ahead, yet it wasn't particularly close. The Nationals went 0 for 10 with runners in scoring position. They had one in each of the first six innings and scratched across a single run. They made two errors, tying their most of the postseason, and Manager Dave Martinez finally made an October decision that backfired.

The Astros, on the other hand, chipped away by getting four runs off starter Aníbal Sánchez in $5\frac{1}{3}$ innings. They benefited because what Martinez had decided, in a critical spot early on, was to keep Sánchez in despite a rare opportunity for the offense to strike. The deficit soon widened with Sánchez on the mound. The Nationals never pretended to close it. That ended their eight-game postseason winning streak — and not so suddenly because it took close to four hours for the Astros to take some momentum back.

"We've lost a game before. Everyone will be okay," first baseman Ryan Zimmerman said. "Nobody thought this was going to be easy, and we have to play good baseball to win."

Little happens quickly in baseball. Games drip by like sand through an hourglass. The season is seven months, if you count spring training, and even longer for a select few. It bends patience before breaking it. The key to winning, above all, is not to go insane.

But the Nationals had arrived back from Houston with great speed. They had turned surviving into a full-on sprint. They entered the weekend with a franchise-best 18-2 record in their past 20 games. They had bullied the Astros in Houston, outscoring them 17-7 in two games, and flipped home-field advantage in their favor. That's how a team replaces long odds with a real, rigid title chance. And that's why a city woke up Friday to host its first World Series game in 86 years.

But what it saw is that the Astros still have a pulse. They didn't stumble to 107 regular season wins. They didn't get all the way here, for the second time in three seasons, by caving when trouble hits. They knocked around Sánchez in the early innings, punching loud outs, pushing ahead with a small rally in the second. Sánchez allowed another run in the third, when Michael Brantley chopped in José Altuve with an infield single, but did keep the Nationals breathing. They just couldn't turn base traffic into results. They wasted back-to-back singles that started the third against Astros starter Zack Greinke. Next they stranded the bases loaded in the fourth.

Astros 4, Nationals 1

HOUSTON	AB	R	H	BI	BB	SO	AVG
Springer cf-rf	4	0	2	0	1	0	.333
Altuve 2b	5	2	2	0	0	0	.400
Brantley lf	4	0	2	2	1	0	.417
Osuna p	0	0	0	0	0	0	---
Bregman 3b	5	0	0	0	0	1	.077
Gurriel 1b	5	0	1	0	0	1	.286
Correa ss	4	1	1	0	0	1	.154
Reddick rf-lf	4	0	1	1	0	0	.111
Chirinos c	4	1	2	1	0	1	.333
Greinke p	1	0	0	0	0	1	.000
James p	0	0	0	0	0	0	---
Tucker ph	0	0	0	0	1	0	.500
Peacock p	0	0	0	0	0	0	---
Harris p	0	0	0	0	0	0	---
Alvarez ph	1	0	0	0	0	0	.429
Smith p	0	0	0	0	0	0	---
Marisnick cf	0	0	0	0	0	0	.000
TOTALS	37	4	11	4	3	5	—

WASHINGTON	AB	R	H	BI	BB	SO	AVG
Turner ss	5	0	1	0	0	1	.231
Eaton rf	4	0	2	0	1	0	.500
Rendon 3b	5	0	1	0	0	0	.154
Soto lf	4	0	0	0	1	3	.364
Cabrera 2b	4	0	2	0	0	1	.385
Zimmerman 1b	3	1	1	0	1	2	.333
Suzuki c	2	0	0	0	0	2	.200
Parra ph	1	0	0	0	0	1	.000
Ross p	0	0	0	0	0	0	---
Kendrick ph	1	0	1	0	0	0	.300
Suero p	0	0	0	0	0	0	---
Robles cf	3	0	1	1	1	1	.200
Sanchez p	2	0	0	0	0	2	.000
Rodney p	0	0	0	0	0	0	---
Adams ph	0	0	0	0	1	0	---
Gomes c	1	0	0	0	0	0	.000
TOTALS	35	1	9	1	5	13	—

HOUSTON	011	011	000	—	4	11	0
WASHINGTON	000	100	000	—	1	9	2

E: Soto (1), Suzuki (1). **LOB:** Houston 10, Washington 12. **2B:** Correa (1), Altuve 2 (3), Rendon (2), Cabrera (1). **3B:** Robles (1). **HR:** Chirinos (1), off Sanchez. **RBI:** Reddick (1), Brantley 2 (2), Chirinos (1), Robles (1). **SB:** Springer 2 (2), Brantley (1), Robles (1). **S:** Greinke. **GIDP:** Robles.
DP: Houston 1 (Bregman, Altuve, Gurriel).

HOUSTON	IP	H	R	ER	BB	SO	NP	ERA
Greinke	4.2	7	1	1	3	6	95	1.93
James	1	0	0	0	0	1	8	6.75
Peacock	0.1	0	0	0	2	1	21	0.00
Harris	1.2	0	0	0	0	2	25	0.00
Smith	1	1	0	0	0	2	18	0.00
Osuna	1	1	0	0	0	1	16	0.00

WASHINGTON	IP	H	R	ER	BB	SO	NP	ERA
Sanchez	5.1	10	4	4	1	4	93	6.75
Rodney	2	0	0	0	2	0	15	0.00
Ross	2	1	0	0	0	0	19	0.00
Suero	1	0	0	0	0	1	9	0.00

WP: James (1-0); **LP:** Sanchez (0-1); **S:** Osuna (1).
Inherited runners-scored: James 2-0, Harris 2-0, Rodney 1-0. **IBB:** off Rodney (Brantley).

The Astros' Carlos Correa scores what would turn out to be the winning run. (Toni L. Sandys/The Washington Post)

"This is what the World Series is about. Like we've talked about before, you have to make the most of opportunities," Eaton said. "When you don't, it's tough sliding."

And it was in the next half-inning that a game of checkers turned into a chess match. The Nationals had another leadoff man aboard once Zimmerman worked a walk. But that meant Sánchez was now coming up in three batters. Any rally would halt with him at the plate. So the bullpen phone rang, and Tanner Rainey began to warm. It seemed that if another player reached, in any way, then Martinez would lift Sánchez for a pinch hitter. But Victor Robles wrinkled a well-laid plan by scoring Zimmerman with a triple.

Sánchez stood between the dugout and plate, looking at Martinez, while the crowd cheered around him. Martinez had a brief discussion with his coaches and told Sánchez to hit for himself. He struck out while trying to bunt, and soon after, Turner ended the threat by rolling a dribbler in front of the plate. Robles bounced 90 feet from home but made it no closer. A pile of missed opportunities grew.

The Astros then tagged Sánchez again in the next half and lent immediate hindsight to Martinez's choice. It kept the Nationals from increasing their scoring chances. But the calculations had to include the volatility of Washington's bullpen. Was Sánchez a better option in the fifth than the erratic Rainey? Who would get loose once Rainey tired? Who would rush into the game if he completely erred?

The last two questions never had to be answered. The only one that mattered, once the late innings arrived, was what happened once Sánchez remained in the game: He recorded just four more outs. He gave up two more runs on a single and Robinson Chirinos's solo homer. And that deficit, in the end, was too much for Washington to overcome.

"I seriously thought about [pinch-hitting]," Martinez said. "But you know what, I liked the way Sánchez was pitching. He only had [65] pitches."

The bats never woke up after that. The Nationals put two runners on in the sixth, on back-to-back walks, but the inning ended without any noise. That was when Turner limped his way to the plate, after fouling a ball off his groin, and promptly struck out. That was when Eaton found new life, boomeranging back into his stance, before he tapped out to first. Those were subtle symbols of an effort that fell flat. They were instances that, across a game full of miscues, were easy to pass off as same old.

But the Nationals can't afford to let this spiral. The Astros have proved, again and again, that an inch of opportunity is more like a gaping hole for them to burst through. And even if the game is slow and nothing's ever decided in one night, a groove can disappear as soon as it arrived. Baseball has no guard against that.

Nats fail at plate, on mound, and series lead vanishes

By Jesse Dougherty

When the energy faded inside Nationals Park, then faded again, and then faded some more, it was replaced, in its entirety, by the feeling that comes when the World Series slips out of a firm grasp.

Washington wasn't used to that before Saturday night. Now it will be, because the Nationals fell to the Houston Astros, 8-1, once their starter faltered and the offense couldn't pick him up. That evened the series at 2-2, back to square one, with the Astros ready to throw their aces the rest of the way.

Patrick Corbin gave up four earned runs in six innings of grinding work. The Nationals' bats were cold for a second consecutive game, managing just four hits, putting each of Corbin's mistakes beneath a microscope.

A Game 3 loss Friday was defined by missed opportunities for the Nationals' offense. This Game 4 loss was marked by generating few opportunities at all. Washington loaded the bases with one out in the sixth and could score only one run. Juan Soto plated it by chopping out to first. Howie Kendrick followed with an inning-ending strikeout. And in the next half-inning, with everything slipping, Houston's Alex Bregman crushed a grand slam off Fernando Rodney. Cheers boomed out of three sections dotting the stadium. They were all filled with Astros fans. The rest of the crowd was quiet, stewing, stacking patience against its sinking guts.

And its silence was loud.

"It's all about perspective," shortstop Trea Turner said. "Now we have a three-game series against the Astros to win the World Series."

This weekend began with a line of kids walking through the Navy Yard neighborhood, just a block from the ballpark, chanting, "Go! … Nats! … Go!" on a cool morning. Nationals banners hung from porches and in storefronts. Nationals talk — lathered in optimism, lacking the restraint of past falls — blared through car radios and restaurant TVs. The city is hosting its first World Series since 1933. That was evident. Then 43,889 people came to see what lies beyond imagination.

But then the Astros took two days to dent the Nationals' runaway faith. Washington had won eight straight, going back to Oct. 7, before Houston had its way against Aníbal Sánchez and the offense flatlined in Game 3. The Nationals went 0 for 10 with runners in scoring position. They were sloppy in the field, making two errors, and it all made Saturday a pivotal turning point.

The on-paper strategy once favored the Nationals, at least before a pitch was thrown. Corbin is a front-line lefty who signed for $140 million this past winter. The Astros turned to 24-year-old Jose Urquidy to begin a bullpen game. It was always the one contest in which Washington would be favored. The Nationals just had to turn logic into results. They couldn't.

"So we have these bats," third baseman Anthony Rendon said, taking one from the top shelf of his locker, talking sarcastically about how the Nationals can improve at the plate. "You try to square it up, and there's a baseball, and then you hit the outfield grass, and usually they are hits."

Urquidy was dominant, throwing five scoreless innings, while Corbin

Astros 8, Nationals 1

HOUSTON	AB	R	H	BI	BB	SO	AVG
Springer rf	4	1	0	0	1	2	.250
Altuve 2b	5	1	2	0	0	0	.400
Brantley lf	5	2	3	0	0	0	.471
Bregman 3b	5	1	3	5	0	0	.222
Gurriel 1b	4	0	1	1	1	2	.278
Correa ss	2	1	0	0	3	0	.133
Chirinos c	5	1	2	2	0	0	.364
Marisnick cf	4	0	2	0	1	1	.400
Urquidy p	2	0	0	0	0	1	.000
James p	0	0	0	0	0	0	—
Harris p	0	0	0	0	0	0	—
Tucker ph	1	1	0	0	1	1	.333
Rondon p	0	0	0	0	0	0	—
Peacock p	0	0	0	0	0	0	—
Alvarez ph	1	0	0	0	0	0	.375
Devenski p	0	0	0	0	0	0	—
TOTALS	38	8	13	8	7	7	—

WASHINGTON	AB	R	H	BI	BB	SO	AVG
Turner ss	5	0	0	0	0	1	.167
Eaton rf	3	0	0	0	1	0	.400
Rendon 3b	4	0	2	0	0	0	.235
Soto lf	3	0	0	1	1	1	.286
Kendrick 2b	4	0	0	0	0	3	.214
Zimmerman 1b	4	0	0	0	0	1	.250
Robles cf	4	0	1	0	0	1	.214
Gomes c	4	0	1	0	0	1	.200
Corbin p	1	0	0	0	0	0	.000
Parra ph	0	1	0	0	1	0	.000
Rainey p	0	0	0	0	0	0	—
Rodney p	0	0	0	0	0	0	—
Suero p	0	0	0	0	0	0	—
Cabrera ph	0	0	0	0	1	0	.385
Guerra p	0	0	0	0	0	0	—
Dozier ph	0	0	0	0	1	0	—
TOTALS	32	1	4	1	5	8	—

HOUSTON	200	200	400	—	8	13	1
WASHINGTON	000	001	000	—	1	4	0

E: Altuve (1). **LOB:** Houston 10, Washington 9. **2B:** Chirinos (1), Gomes (1). **HR:** Chirinos (2), off Corbin; Bregman (2), off Rodney. **RBI:** Bregman 5 (7), Gurriel (3), Chirinos 2 (3), Soto (4). **SB:** Marisnick (1). **DP:** Washington 1 (Rendon, Zimmerman).

HOUSTON	IP	H	R	ER	BB	SO	NP	ERA
Urquidy	5	2	0	0	4	0	67	0.00
James	1	0	1	1	2	1	15	10.8
Harris	0.2	1	0	0	0	1	7	0.00
Rondon	2	1	0	0	1	0	20	0.00
Peacock	1.1	0	0	0	1	1	32	0.00
Devenski	1	0	0	0	1	1	18	4.50

WASHINGTON	IP	H	R	ER	BB	SO	NP	ERA
Corbin	6	7	4	4	2	5	96	5.14
Rainey	1	0	2	2	2	0	13	16.2
Rodney	1	2	2	2	3	0	25	9.00
Suero	1	0	0	0	0	1	5	0.00
Guerra	2	4	0	0	0	1	27	3.00

WP: Urquidy (1-0); **LP:** Corbin (0-1). **Inherited runners-scored:** Harris 2-1, Peacock 2-0, Rodney 2-2, Suero 3-0. **T:** 3:48. **A:** 43,889 (41,313).

Fernando Rodney exits after giving up a grand slam to Alex Bregman in a rough seventh inning. (Jonathan Newton/The Washington Post)

couldn't hold the Astros down. Corbin was tagged for two runs in the first, on four straight hits, and his pitch count spiked to 26. The Astros turned two get-me-over sinkers into singles. He couldn't locate his slider, his best pitch, and slipped again when Robinson Chirinos lifted a two-run shot off him in the fourth.

It was Chirinos who bounced into a double play to help Corbin escape the first. Before that at-bat, with Corbin struggling, pitching coach Paul Menhart walked to the mound for a short conference. Corbin followed by throwing Chirinos two change-ups, a pitch he typically uses just 5 percent of the time, and soon retired him with an inside sinker. So, in their second matchup, Corbin attacked Chirinos with his ninth change-up of the outing. It fluttered into the heart of the zone, like a one-winged bird, looking ready to be swatted. Then it flew high over the stadium and landed deep in the left field seats.

"The location on that pitch wasn't where I wanted it. It was right down the middle," Corbin said, adding that he wanted it down and away. "If I locate it better, it's a different outcome."

Chirinos slapped his chest while skipping toward home plate. Corbin stood by the mound, some 60 feet away, his shoulders slumped and his face blank. He is known for handling big moments with a personality that doesn't even quiver. But that has been absent for four of his seven playoff appearances. He is the first player in history to make three starts and four relief appearances in the same postseason. If his arm is tiring, and the workload is too big, he probably would never say. It just lengthens the list of problems Washington has to solve. And fast.

Rotation depth was supposed to separate the Nationals in this series. The offense came up big in Houston. But Corbin wilted, the bats did, too, and the Astros widened the gap when Tanner Rainey and Rodney shrank in the seventh inning. Manager Dave Martinez turned to Rainey, then Rodney, to hold a three-run deficit in place, even though he had Sean Doolittle and Daniel Hudson sitting in the bullpen after two full days of rest.

The decision backfired when Rainey couldn't find the strike zone, Rodney couldn't avoid hard contact, and, after Bregman's blast and five walks in the inning, the deficit ballooned.

"We've been doing this all season," Corbin said. "We've had losses, big losses, and bounced back fine. Guys will be ready to go tomorrow."

The Nationals have scored just twice through 18 innings in their own ballpark. They are 1 for 19 with runners in scoring position across those two games. The lone hit did not even plate a run. They are picking the worst time to dig up old habits — a lifeless bullpen, poor situational hitting, caving in October — and will now face Gerrit Cole, Justin Verlander and, maybe, Zack Greinke with their title shot back in the balance.

Their saving grace is that Max Scherzer and Stephen Strasburg will be on the mound for the next two games. The only way to swallow Saturday was to remember, somehow, that the Astros did all this to catch up.

Hitters are lost, ace is out, and hopes hang by a thread

By Jesse Dougherty

It didn't matter that Joe Ross kept the Washington Nationals within a reasonable distance of the Houston Astros on Sunday night. It didn't matter that the bullpen did, too, altering a season-long narrative that leads balloon whenever relievers touch the mound. It didn't matter when there were 12 outs left for the Nationals, then nine, then six, then, all of a sudden, one became zero, and the World Series swung to Houston, where only a dwindling title chance awaits.

None of it mattered because, in the end, the Nationals still aren't hitting. They fell to the Astros, 7-1, after Gerrit Cole gave up one run in seven innings. They fell after Ross, a late fill-in for Max Scherzer because of neck spasms and nerve irritation, allowed four runs in five frames. They fell after Juan Soto's solo homer in the seventh, a towering shot, was the only way they could scratch the scoreboard.

The Nationals collected just four hits against 11 strikeouts. Their 2-0 series lead evaporated in their ballpark, then became a 3-2 deficit because they scored three runs across three contests in Washington. No team has taken the World Series with four victories on the road. Now the Nationals' only remaining chance is to become the first.

"What's new? That's kind of our feeling. What's new?" right fielder Adam Eaton said. "Backs against the wall. Winners come to play when their backs are against the wall."

Scherzer knew in the early afternoon, before even leaving for the ballpark, that there was no way he could pitch. He couldn't move his right arm when he woke up. He needed his wife, Erica, to help him get dressed. The hope is that he could pitch Game 7 on Wednesday if the Nationals make it there. That will hinge on his neck responding to a cortisone shot, injected Sunday, that's supposed to alleviate the nerve irritation in 48 hours.

"I'm as disappointed as I possibly can be not to be able to pitch tonight," Scherzer said in the afternoon, about two hours before the first pitch, as Ross was down the hall preparing for the biggest start of his life. "It's Game 5 of the World Series."

The show had to go on. It always does. Ross spent the season bouncing between the majors and minors, between the rotation and bullpen, between being injured and in the Nationals' plans. Now he walked into a sold-out stadium at 7:39 p.m., his eyes fixed straight ahead, while the crowd gave him a long, loud standing ovation. Fans chanted "Let's go, Joe!" as game time neared. This was Ross's third postseason performance — a short start in 2016, then a two-inning relief appearance Friday — and the crowd was ready for him.

The problem was that the Astros were, too. And the even bigger problem, eventually, was that the offense never showed up.

"That's one of the best lineups in baseball," Ross said of his uneven performance. "I'm not going to expect myself to strike out 20 like Max does, you know? Just stick to my game."

Astros 7, Nationals 1

HOUSTON	AB	R	H	BI	BB	SO	AVG
Springer cf-rf	3	2	2	2	2	0	.316
Altuve 2b	5	0	1	0	0	0	.360
Brantley rf-lf	3	0	0	0	1	0	.400
Bregman 3b	4	0	0	0	0	0	.182
Gurriel 1b	4	1	2	1	0	0	.318
Alvarez lf	3	2	3	2	0	0	.545
Marisnick pr-cf	1	0	0	0	0	1	.333
Correa ss	4	1	1	2	0	1	.158
Maldonado c	3	1	1	0	1	0	.286
Cole p	3	0	0	0	0	1	.000
Smith p	0	0	0	0	0	0	—
Tucker ph	1	0	0	0	0	1	.250
Pressly p	0	0	0	0	0	0	—
TOTALS	**34**	**7**	**10**	**7**	**4**	**4**	**—**

WASHINGTON	AB	R	H	BI	BB	SO	AVG
Turner ss	4	0	0	0	0	1	.136
Eaton rf	4	0	0	0	0	2	.316
Rendon 3b	3	0	0	0	1	0	.200
Soto lf	4	1	2	1	0	1	.333
Kendrick 2b-1b	4	0	1	0	0	1	.222
Zimmerman 1b	2	0	0	0	1	1	.222
Hudson p	0	0	0	0	0	0	—
Suero p	0	0	0	0	0	0	—
Robles cf	3	0	0	0	0	2	.176
Gomes c	3	0	1	0	0	0	.250
Ross p	1	0	0	0	0	1	.000
Rainey p	0	0	0	0	0	0	—
Parra ph	1	0	0	0	0	1	.000
Doolittle p	0	0	0	0	0	0	—
Cabrera 2b	1	0	0	0	0	1	.357
TOTALS	**30**	**1**	**4**	**1**	**2**	**11**	**—**

HOUSTON						
HOUSTON	020	200	012	—	7	10 0
WASHINGTON	000	000	100	—	1	4 0

LOB: Houston 4, Washington 4. **2B:** Springer (2).
HR: Alvarez (1), off Ross; Correa (1), off Ross; Springer (2), off Hudson; Soto (2), off Cole. **RBI:** Alvarez 2 (2), Correa 2 (2), Gurriel (4), Springer 2 (4), Soto (5).
DP: Houston 1 (Correa, Altuve, Gurriel); Washington 3 (Turner, Kendrick, Zimmerman; Kendrick, Turner, Zimmerman; Rendon, Kendrick, Zimmerman).

HOUSTON	IP	H	R	ER	BB	SO	NP	ERA
Cole	7	3	1	1	2	9	110	3.86
Smith	1	1	0	0	0	1	16	0.00
Pressly	1	0	0	0	0	1	13	16.2

WASHINGTON	IP	H	R	ER	BB	SO	NP	ERA
Ross	5	5	4	4	2	1	78	5.14
Rainey	1	0	0	0	0	0	9	10.1
Doolittle	1	1	0	0	1	1	14	0.00
Hudson	1.2	4	3	3	1	2	36	12.0
Suero	1	0	0	0	0	0	2	0.00

WP: Cole (1-1); **LP:** Ross (0-1).
IBB: off Hudson (Brantley). **WP:** Ross.
T: 3:19. **A:** 43,910 (41,313).

Nationals players and fans watch the closing moments of Game 5. (Jonathan Newton / The Washington Post)

It's not that Houston was all over Ross. It was just that his final line was stained, forever, by two decisive swings. The first was by Yordan Alvarez, the Astros' 22-year-old slugger, a tall lefty who had yet to find his power stroke in the postseason. That changed when he lined a low-and-away fastball over the wall in left-center to score Yuli Gurriel and himself. It was his first homer since Sept. 21. The second cut was Carlos Correa's, in the fourth, when Ross was one pitch away from escaping another inning.

He worked Correa to 0-2 and threw him a biting slider at the knees. It looked like a strike until, at the last nanosecond, it dived out of the zone. Yet Correa didn't flinch. Instead, four pitches later, the shortstop smacked a hanging slider for a two-run blast. Correa stared at the ball before lightly dropping his bat into the dirt. Ross gave it a glance, as if he didn't want to see, and held up his glove to get another ball from catcher Yan Gomes.

"As far as baseball goes, something small happens, and it seems like, later that at-bat, always something big follows up," Ross said of not getting a close call on that outside slider. "So unfortunate that's how it went, but nothing I can do about it now."

Ross, in the end, couldn't do enough to give this flatlined offense a chance. It would be hard for any pitcher to, really, given how little run support there has been since the Nationals got back to Washington. It is tough to blame a team for wilting against Cole, maybe baseball's best pitcher, the most dominant ace in a matchup chock-full of them. The Nationals beat him in Game 1. But the Astros have not lost back-to-back Cole starts since April 20 and 25. They are since 28-4 when he pitches, counting this game, yet the issue was what the Nationals did at the plate — or didn't do — across the 27 innings here.

They managed just 17 total hits in Games 3, 4 and 5. They combined to go 1 for 21 with runners in scoring position. Soto's homer, his second off Cole in the series, was too little, too late, and soon their last threat ended with Victor Robles leaping out of the batter's box in frustration.

Robles was Cole's final batter, and they wrestled into a full count with two down in the seventh. Cole came with a high fastball, and thinking it was ball four, Robles started toward first. It was off the outside corner. But umpire Lance Barksdale signaled for a strikeout, and close to 44,000 people couldn't believe it. The whole stadium booed. There were screams from the dugout. Robles backpedaled halfway up the first base line, yelling at Barksdale, then lobbed his helmet and batting gloves back toward the plate.

It was that kind of night for the Nationals. It was that kind of weekend. And it will soon become clear whether a bad three days — a really bad three days — are what will finally do this team in.

Strasburg dominates, Nats force a Game 7

Manager Dave Martinez argues with umpires in the seventh inning. (Jonathan Newton/The Washington Post)

By Jesse Dougherty

What it took for the Washington Nationals to play again, to have one last chance at a dream that has wavered back into focus, was 25 outs from Stephen Strasburg, a lined homer from Adam Eaton, a towering homer from Juan Soto, the sidestepping of a controversial call from the umpires — when Trea Turner was ruled out for, well, running to first base — and a two-run homer lofted into the left field seats by Anthony Rendon.

That was it. And now they have a shot to win the World Series in Houston on Wednesday night.

When it was all added up Tuesday and the Nationals kept stretching fate, they beat the Houston Astros, 7-2, to force a Game 7 at Minute Maid Park. Strasburg allowed just two runs, both in the first, in $8^1/_3$ dominant innings. Eaton went yard in the fifth, Soto homered two batters later, and Rendon later hit a homer and a double to collect five RBI and provide breathing room. Washington has now won four elimination games this October and, with that, will fight for as long as the calendar allows.

The Nationals' season — their comeback from a 19-31 record in May, their sprint through the playoffs and this clash with the Astros — will come down to one game Wednesday night. It will decide everything. And it will start, for the Nationals, with Max Scherzer on the mound.

"This is what you live for," Scherzer said after the Game 6 victory. "For me, I am in my pregame routine now. That's where I'm just at mentally. Here we go."

The Nationals felt they needed just one good bounce — a bloop single, an Astros error, anything — to turn this series back around. They left Houston with a two-game lead last week, closing in on history, carrying belief. Then they returned in a hole, trailing 3-2, trying like mad to slow the Astros and start their engine again. But now they had Strasburg on the mound. They had won all four elimination games he had pitched in, going back to 2016, and it was fitting that he went out and nearly tossed his third career complete game. These Nationals will ride their rotation until the end.

And it was Strasburg who, not two weeks ago, best summed up Washington's sprint through the postseason. In the clubhouse after Game 4 of the National League Championship Series, after the Nationals had clinched a World Series berth, Strasburg looked at the beer-soaked floor and squinted. He considered why some teams get a title chance and others don't. That's when this thought popped into his head: "You have a great year, and you can run into a buzz saw. Maybe this year we are the buzz saw."

He was right for another two games. He was wrong when the series swung against Washington. Then the Nationals came back to Houston, where they have yet to lose and again looked like the team no one wants to face. He allowed two runs in the first as Houston erased the Nationals' first lead but quickly settled into an unshakable groove. The Astros were only in his way. Then it was only a matter of time before the Nationals' offense, the same one that managed just three runs across three home losses, used Strasburg's effort as a springboard.

"We've been groomed for elimination games because we've played quite a few of them," Strasburg said, speaking for his team but sounding as if he were assessing himself. "There were some regular games there, too, that you could consider elimination games."

They silenced the Astros' crowd with a pair of fifth-inning swings, first on Eaton's solo homer and then with Soto's before he mimicked Alex

Nationals 7, Astros 2

WASHINGTON	AB	R	H	BI	BB	SO	AVG
Turner ss	5	2	2	0	0	0	.185
Eaton rf	2	2	1	1	1	0	.333
Rendon 3b	4	1	3	5	1	0	.292
Soto lf	5	1	1	1	0	0	.304
Kendrick dh	4	0	1	0	0	0	.227
Cabrera 2b	4	0	0	0	0	2	.278
Zimmerman 1b	3	0	0	0	1	2	.190
Robles cf	4	0	0	0	0	3	.143
Gomes c	4	1	1	0	0	1	.250
TOTALS	**35**	**7**	**9**	**7**	**3**	**8**	**—**

HOUSTON	AB	R	H	BI	BB	SO	AVG
Springer cf	4	1	2	0	0	1	.348
Altuve 2b	3	0	0	1	0	1	.321
Brantley lf	4	0	0	0	0	0	.333
Bregman 3b	4	1	2	1	0	0	.231
Gurriel 1b	3	0	0	0	1	0	.280
Alvarez dh	3	0	0	0	1	0	.429
Correa ss	4	0	1	0	0	2	.174
Chirinos c	4	0	0	0	0	2	.267
Reddick rf	3	0	1	0	0	1	.167
TOTALS	**32**	**2**	**6**	**2**	**2**	**7**	**—**

WASHINGTON	100	020	202	—	7	9	0
HOUSTON	200	000	000	—	2	6	0

LOB: Washington 6, Houston 6. **2B:** Turner (1), Rendon (3), Springer 2 (4), Correa (2). **HR:** Eaton (2), off Verlander; Soto (3), off Verlander; Rendon (1), off Harris; Bregman (3), off Strasburg. **RBI:** Rendon 5 (7), Eaton (4), Soto (6), Altuve (1), Bregman (8). **SF:** Altuve. **S:** Eaton.

WASHINGTON	IP	H	R	ER	BB	SO	NP	ERA
Strasburg	8.1	5	2	2	2	7	104	2.51
Doolittle	2	1	0	0	0	0	11	0.00

HOUSTON	IP	H	R	ER	BB	SO	NP	ERA
Verlander	5	5	3	3	3	3	93	5.73
Peacock	1.1	1	1	1	0	2	21	3.00
Harris	2	1	1	1	0	0	5	2.25
Pressly	1	0	0	0	0	2	14	10.1
Devenski	1	2	2	2	0	1	22	9.00

WP: Strasburg, (2-0); **LP:** Verlander, (0-2). **Inherited runners-scored:** Harris 1-1. **HBP:** Devenski (Eaton). **WP:** Strasburg. **T:** 3:37. **A:** 43,384 (41,168).

After allowing two runs in the first inning, Stephen Strasburg shut down the Astros into the ninth. (Toni L. Sandys/The Washington Post)

Bregman by carrying his bat all the way to first base. Then the game went totally sideways in the seventh. Turner hit a dribbler in front of the mound and took off toward first. He was a step from the base, and mid-stride, when Brad Peacock hit him with an offline throw. Turner advanced to second, Yan Gomes to third, and that put two runners in scoring position with no outs.

But Sam Holbrook, the home plate umpire, signaled Turner out for interference. Washington Manager Dave Martinez began screaming, the veins popping from his neck, his fists balled up as he pushed onto his toes for more volume. The call was confirmed after a long discussion. Turner stood at the lip of the dugout, staring at the crew, stepping onto the field before his teammates moved in the way to calm him down. And by the end of the top half of the inning, even after Rendon eased the drama by parking a Will Harris cutter in the seats, Martinez was ejected for continuing to argue Holbrook's ruling.

But Strasburg smoothed out the rest of Martinez's

pitching plan. He completed a gem at 104 pitches. He handed the ball to Sean Doolittle, to leave no doubt, and the southpaw shut the door. And so the Nationals kept on breathing.

"Sometimes your big guys step up when they need to," Howie Kendrick said of Strasburg and Rendon. "And tonight our guys stepped up for us."

This sport, when stripped of its nuances, when whittled down to size, is really just a constant search for one more. Pitchers work for hours, staring at video, leafing through scouting reports, even losing sleep, to throw one more strike. Batters stay in the cage, swinging until their hands sting, swearing they're almost done, to find one more hit. Teams are no different, once individuals become a whole, once those hours add up to a season, and all that matters is earning one more chance.

So there were the Washington Nationals on Tuesday, in the twilight of October, boiling eight months of work into a final, simple task: They have to win one more game. That's it.

No doubt, just hope for team that wouldn't die

Howie Kendrick hits a two-run homer
in the seventh inning to give the Nationals
a lead they would not relinquish.
(John McDonnell/The Washington Post)

By Barry Svrluga

In the end, one last time, they were dead and found life. What was this, the 33rd time that happened this month — one for each of the summers Washington went without baseball? The parade route through downtown Houston had been mapped out, and the Washington Nationals reoriented it to the northeast, to Constitution Avenue. They travel with defibrillators and don't care how often they use them.

Wednesday night, in the seventh game of the World Series, the doctors on call were Anthony Rendon and Howie Kendrick. They'll be remembered in the District — and well beyond — for the seventh-inning home runs that turned yet another certain loss into yet another improbable win. But if anyone wants to single them out, they'll call in the rest of the Nationals who finished the Houston Astros with a 6-2 victory Wednesday night, because over the course of a rollicking summer and an inconceivable October, this team danced together, this team hugged each other, this team won as one.

"That's what we've done all year," said first baseman Ryan Zimmerman, the longest-tenured player. "What a group of guys. It's unbelievable. Everything I could have imagined — and more."

Let your mouth form the words and sing it out loud: The Washington Nationals won the World Series. Repeating that sentence is allowed. Say it enough, and some day it may even feel normal.

That day, though, wasn't Wednesday night at Minute Maid Park, where the Nationals trailed the Astros 2-0 in the seventh inning. That deficit, written in black and white, doesn't seem daunting. In Game 7, it felt gaping.

"The impact, the magnitude, it kind of felt more than what it actually was," Rendon said. "But it was still [2-0]. We knew we were still in the game. We didn't doubt each other."

How to doubt a group that was 19-31 in May yet played the final game of the World Series? There was a wild-card victory in which they trailed in the eighth inning, a division series in which they needed to win the final two games, and the sixth game of this series, in which they trailed in the fifth. So by Wednesday, we had learned what this team was about. There is no doubt. There is only hope.

"That's how this group plays," General Manager Mike Rizzo said. "Even when things were bad, even when it seemed like there was no way out back in the spring, they were total pros. They never wavered. They had something special."

Even before the homers from Rendon and Kendrick — not to mention Patrick Corbin's brilliant outing in relief — that was obvious about this team. They won the World Series, Washington's second, joining only the 1924 Senators. More importantly, they transformed what their town — which watched those Senators relocate twice — believes is possible from its baseball team. Having baseball back doesn't mean there's only pain. Having it back can bring bliss.

From 2006 to 2010, the Nationals lost 91, 89, 102, 103 and 93 games, respectively. Losing seemed ingrained. The World Series was a television program.

And then the 2012 team broke through with a division title. The growth was slow. The pivot — in both expectations and possibilities — seemed sudden.

"You're really talking about '08 to '12, so four years of growth for an organization to then be expected to make the playoffs," Zimmerman said. "And then all of a sudden, if you don't get past the first round of the playoffs, you're a huge disappointment. So it all happened kind of fast."

Which makes Wednesday night, and the month that led to it, hard to process in the moment or even overnight. So much was accomplished over October, what with four previous games when a loss meant welcome to winter. Instead, they won, and extended fall.

Nationals 6, Astros 2

WASHINGTON	AB	R	H	BI	BB	SO	AVG
Turner ss	4	0	0	0	1	1	.161
Eaton rf	4	1	1	2	1	0	.320
Rendon 3b	5	1	1	1	0	1	.276
Soto lf	4	1	2	1	1	1	.333
Kendrick dh	3	1	2	2	1	0	.280
Cabrera 2b	3	0	1	0	0	0	.286
Zimmerman 1b	3	0	1	0	1	0	.208
Gomes c	4	1	0	0	0	0	.188
Robles cf	4	1	1	0	0	0	.160
TOTALS	34	6	9	6	5	3	—

HOUSTON	AB	R	H	BI	BB	SO	AVG
Springer cf-rf	4	0	0	0	0	1	.296
Altuve 2b	5	0	1	0	0	1	.303
Brantley lf	4	0	1	0	1	1	.321
Bregman 3b	3	0	0	0	1	1	.207
Gurriel 1b	4	2	2	1	0	0	.310
Alvarez dh	3	0	1	0	1	0	.412
Correa ss	4	0	2	1	0	1	.222
Chirinos c	4	0	0	0	0	2	.211
Reddick rf	2	0	1	0	0	0	.214
Marisnick ph-cf	2	0	1	0	0	1	.375
TOTALS	35	2	9	2	4	8	—

WASHINGTON	000	000	312 —	6 9 0
HOUSTON	010	010	000 —	2 9 1

E: Marisnick (1). **LOB:** Washington 7, Houston 10. **HR:** Rendon (2), off Greinke; Kendrick (1), off Harris; Gurriel (1), off Scherzer. **RBI:** Rendon (8), Kendrick 2 (3), Soto (7), Eaton 2 (6), Gurriel (5), Correa (3). **SB:** Eaton (1). **S:** Cabrera.
DP: Washington 1 (Cabrera, Zimmerman); Houston 1 (Altuve, Gurriel).

WASHINGTON	IP	H	R	ER	BB	SO	NP	ERA
Scherzer	5	7	2	2	4	3	103	3.60
Corbin	3	2	0	0	0	3	44	3.60
Hudson	1	0	0	0	0	2	12	9.00

HOUSTON	IP	H	R	ER	BB	SO	NP	ERA
Greinke	6.1	2	2	2	2	3	80	2.45
Harris	0	2	1	1	0	0	5	4.50
Osuna	1.1	2	1	1	2	0	36	3.86
Pressly	1	0	0	0	0	0	2	9.00
Smith	1	2	2	2	1	0	15	5.40
Urquidy	2	1	0	0	0	0	10	0.00

WP: Corbin (1-1); **LP:** Harris (0-1).
Inherited runners-scored: Harris 1-1, Osuna 1-0, Pressly 2-0, Urquidy 3-2.
T: 3:42. **A:** 43,326 (41,168).

Fans didn't let the rain douse their joy at the watch party for Game 7 at Nationals Park. (Katherine Frey/The Washington Post)

So to the seventh inning of Game 7. Given everything that happened from then on, try to remember how dead the Nationals felt to that point. Zack Greinke, the veteran Houston right-hander, looked as if he controlled the ball on a string. Through six innings, Washington's offense against him: Juan Soto's second-inning single and Kendrick's fifth-inning walk.

"Just try to keep on going," Rendon said.

"What choice did we have?" Zimmerman said. "It's the last game."

The miracle, to that point, was that Houston's lead was only 2-0. Max Scherzer tried to shake off a neck issue that had cost him his scheduled start in Game 5. He was nothing if not game, but his stuff was not good. Combine nine Astros left on base through five innings with Greinke's easy mastery, and a 2-0 game somehow felt like it was 7-0.

"But these guys, they're confident, they really are," Manager Dave Martinez said. "And they don't lose that confidence or that focus regardless of the situation."

No one more so than Rendon, their flatlining superstar. It was Rendon who had pushed the Nats to Wednesday night with a two-run homer in Game 6. It was Rendon who could get them back in it in Game 7. Only the strongest stethoscope can detect his pulse.

"Things are going crazy," Rizzo said, "and he's yawning in the batter's box."

So, then, ho-hum, Greinke's 1-0 change-up sent out to left field. Life, where there was none.

His heroics meant nothing if Kendrick didn't follow them up. "He was my pick to click," Rendon said. After Greinke walked Soto, in came Will Harris. Kendrick got an 0-1 cutter. He clicked — and clanked it off the foul pole in right.

The lead now in hand, Kendrick raced back to the dugout to dance. The home run was for the guys right there, of course. For Strasburg, whose masterpiece in Game 6 helped propel them here. For Adam Eaton, who couldn't wait to shift gears in a pretend car at Kendrick's side on the bench. For Zimmerman, the franchise leader in every meaningful category, often described as its face, but also its conscience and soul. For all of them.

Now that it's done, remember not just that they won but how they won. The 2019 Washington Nationals taught us all lessons — about patience and belief, about faith and fortitude, about finding life where none seemed to exist. They are champions because of all of that, even if — right now or next month or next year — it's unfathomable they did it at all.

Nationals' league

In his 15th season with the Nationals, Ryan Zimmerman reached
the World Series for the first time. (Toni L. Sandys/The Washington Post)

By Thomas Boswell

What the Washington Nationals have done this season is like going into your backyard with a spade to plant petunias and, instead, striking oil.

Their appointment with the World Series, just 14 days after facing elimination in the wild-card game, is like spilling water on Grandma's painting of an old farmhouse and finding out she had painted over a still-pristine Picasso.

The Nats' pennant-winning, 7-4 victory over the St. Louis Cardinals in Game 4 of the National League Championship Series on Tuesday night began as a massive gleeful party, constructed on an amazing seven-run first inning that had a crowd of 43,976 attempting to prove that mass delirium is possible. For two hours, Nationals Park witnessed a romantic comedy: Town loves team, team loves town, and the Cardinals roll over and play dead to end this four-game sweep.

But by the late innings, this game — even with a huge NLCS lead — felt like a zombie slasher meets Frankenstein's bigger brother as closer Daniel Hudson escaped a bases-loaded eighth-inning jam by getting Matt Carpenter, the go-ahead run, to ground out.

In the end, the bullpen of Tanner Rainey, Sean Doolittle and Hudson held the fort for the last dozen outs — a plot twist almost beyond comprehension for one of the worst bullpens in 50 years. But it was the fitting ending in a year when the Nats tweaked, fixed or worked around every problem.

That such a bullpen would now stand tall just fits the whole season-long theme: There is no gift like the unexpected gift, no joy like the jubilation when the next emotion you anticipated was sadness.

"Some of the best things come from the unexpected moments," said postseason hero Howie Kendrick, who was named the NLCS MVP.

There is no shock like the discovery that a desperate moment — May 23 for these Nats — that felt like the end of an era of success was really a time of transformation under duress into something better, richer and more satisfying than you had imagined possible.

Just when it felt like the best era of Washington baseball since 1924 to 1933 was swirling down the drain, with the Nats' record at 19-31, suddenly everything that seemed wrong began to go right.

The struggling and lame — Trea Turner, Anthony Rendon and Juan Soto — came back from the injured list and got hot. The team landed a Baby Shark named Gerardo Parra on a one-ounce test line — picked up free, with the San Francisco Giants still paying his salary. And the team that knows how to put the huge, ugly "E" in "elimination game" became the first team in major league history to win two of them in the same October after trailing by three or more runs.

The Nationals — once known as the "Natinals" on their own jerseys, the same team that got knocked out of the first round of the playoffs four times — celebrated the patriarch of D.C. baseball by claiming the pennant on Ted Lerner's 94th birthday. His team knows what it has given him. And he understands what he has given to this city for the first time in 86 years.

"I want to tell the fans, 'This is for you!'" Lerner said in the postgame celebration.

"We earned the 12 games under .500 [in May]. We were bad," said General Manager Mike Rizzo, ripping off a list of all of his team's early-season sins and injuries. "But we also earned the [.675 winning percentage] the rest of the way."

The Nats go to the World Series as just what they love to be — disregarded, constantly underdogs. They will face an American League champion, the Houston Astros or New York Yankees, that will be regarded as much their superior. But the Nats are certain in their baseball guts that this will be darn close to a toss-up World Series.

"These guys back here, they cured my heart," said Manager Dave Martinez, his face split with grins after being rushed from a game to the hospital just four weeks ago with what he feared was a heart attack.

Two points, both apparent in Game 4, should be made about these Nats — akin to noting that lightning can not only electrocute you but also knock down trees on your head.

In their past 123 games, the Nationals have scored more runs per game than every team but the Yankees. The Nats' lineup, in their current state of perfect health, is one of the deepest and most multifaceted in the majors.

Game 4's seven-run first inning epitomized the Nats' versatile attack — one that's out of step with the home-run-or-whiff model of this era. Yes, the Nats hit homers — 231, but that was only 13th best this year. Within the NL, they were first in on-base percentage, tied for first in batting average and second in fewest strikeouts. They also tied for the league lead in steals. To many, all of this is heresy. But it has worked, with a master-class example in the first inning.

The Nats scored seven runs without hitting a ball farther than 275 feet in the air. They slapped a single (Turner) and double (Soto) to the opposite field. A power hitter (Rendon) put the first pitch he saw in play because he knew it could produce a sacrifice fly. Two players merely put the ball in play: Ryan Zimmerman sharply and Victor Robles with a popup. The Cardinals made an error on the first and completely missed the second as it fell among three of them. Yan Gomes and Turner followed with two-run singles drilled through the left side of the infield. Between them, pitcher Patrick Corbin put down a perfect sacrifice bunt.

It was, frankly, nothing less than baseball high art: The first 10 hitters of a game with the pennant on the line executed perfectly.

Dakota Hudson, the Cardinals' wins leader, left having gotten one — o-n-e — out.

The other Nats weapon that has brought them to this city-delighting pennant is depth. In World Series games played in the AL city, the Nats will be able to pick a bat off their loaded bench to be the designated hitter — perhaps switch-hitting Asdrúbal Cabrera (91 RBI), or Brian Dozier or Matt Adams (20 homers each). There might even be a spot for Parra — who got a hit, to universal delight, in the pennant clincher.

In the glee that now sweeps over Washington, don't bet the house on the Nats beating the 107-win Astros or 103-win Yankees. But it might be worth taking out a second mortgage on your gardening shed.

Whatever ills or joys are still to come, Tuesday night was the best baseball victory in D.C. since 1933, another era when America seemed chest-deep in serious problems. In October 2019, Washington is united behind one flag and one purpose — symbolized by those silly Baby Shark bandannas.

The Nats are also a team for their place and time. They exalt in their diversity with eight key players, and team leaders, from Venezuela, Brazil and the Dominican Republic. Martinez told his Latin teammates when he arrived in the minors in 1983, "Sorry, but I don't speak Spanish."

Now, of course, he does. But he has also learned a lot about another language that he struggled with when he took the job last year: He is closer to fluent in "bullpen." He has learned at least four words — Doolittle, Hudson, Rainey and Rodney. And he used that vocabulary well in Game 4, getting a scoreless inning from Rainey in the sixth. Doolittle blanked the Cardinals in the seventh, and Hudson completed a scary eighth before a perfect ninth to end it.

All of these factors are part of the explanation of why the Nats' NL championship is neither magic nor fluke. It is excellent, but some of it hides in plain sight.

This, however, is also a team with a fire deep inside that it seldom fully articulates. This is a band of old men without rings.

Only one National, reliever Hunter Strickland, has played for a World Series winner. After Game 2, Zimmerman and Max Scherzer, both 35, referred to themselves, and the 16 other Nats on this playoff roster who are past their 30th birthdays, as "Los Viejos" — the Old Men.

"Everybody wants to forget the old guys," said a jubilant, hat-backward Scherzer amid the infield celebration. "Well, we went out and won the National League pennant!"

For Washington, it has seemed as if it took a baseball eternity to win a pennant. But to three-quarters of these Nationals, winning the NLCS may mean more than just the D.C. joyride of a visit to the World Series.

To them, grabbing a pennant, marvelous as that is for their city and its fans, is probably — though none will say it — a steppingstone to their collective dream of rings.

If you think Game 4 was hard as that 7-0 lead dwindled to 7-4, and that those comebacks in elimination games against the Milwaukee Brewers and Los Angeles Dodgers were harrowing, be forewarned. What these old men, plus a few gifted youngsters, with their dugout dancing and hugging, really have in mind, starting next Tuesday, will be even more challenging. Perhaps even impossible.

But, as we have learned, the prize that is least expected, the goal that seems almost impossible, is also the most thrilling.

Pop the corks. Raise the pennant. But know one thing: The Nationals don't think their season has reached its peak.

Sánchez flirts with no-hitter in opener

Aníbal Sánchez allowed one hit
in 7⅔ scoreless innings.
(Jonathan Newton/The Washington Post)

By Jesse Dougherty

Some St. Louis Cardinals fans even clapped — because how could they not? — when Aníbal Sánchez was finally finished carving through their team at Busch Stadium on Friday night.

Sánchez came four outs away from throwing the third postseason no-hitter in baseball history. Instead, in a consolation he would certainly take, the 35-year-old righty led the Washington Nationals to a 2-0 victory over the St. Louis Cardinals. He gave up one hit and four base-runners in $7^2/_3$ innings. He got the game to Sean Doolittle, avoiding the Nationals' middle relievers altogether, and the lefty retired all four batters he faced out of the bullpen.

And that effort, when totaled up, gave Washington a 1-0 lead in its first National League Championship Series.

"It's good when I got that kind of command," Sánchez said, and that was the only part of his performance that was understated. "Because it's easier for the catcher to call the game."

Sánchez was on the mound because of what it took for the Nationals to get here. They needed everything Max Scherzer, Stephen Strasburg and Patrick Corbin could offer to beat the Milwaukee Brewers in the wild-card game, then Los Angeles Dodgers in the NL Division Series. They needed 224 pitches from Strasburg, the most of any pitcher in the divisional round, and 200 from Scherzer. Each made one of his three appearances out of the bullpen. Corbin made two in relief, with mixed results, and tossed 107 pitches in a Game 1 start. Dave Martinez managed as if his life depended on every out. And it worked.

But he couldn't do that against the Cardinals. He didn't expect to plug Scherzer or Strasburg or Corbin into the late innings. The NLCS is more reflective of the regular season, as Scherzer noted Friday, and so Sánchez started with a shorthanded bullpen behind him. Closer Daniel Hudson remained in Phoenix following the birth of his third daughter. The Nationals were also down catcher Kurt Suzuki and center fielder Victor Robles, two everyday players, because of injuries. It made it fair to favor the Cardinals in the opener, if only slightly, if only because Washington's lineup and late relief were thinned.

Then Sánchez flipped that logic on its head.

"I probably would have bet on him fourth," General Manager Mike Rizzo said, with a laugh, of which of his starters he would have guessed would flirt with a playoff no-hitter. That's because it's easy to cast aside Sánchez in a near $95 million rotation stacked with Scherzer, Strasburg and Corbin. But he has now allowed just one run in $12^2/_3$ innings this postseason. And, in the larger picture, he's been rock solid since returning from the injured list in mid-May.

He continued that with his best command in the early innings Friday. His low-90s fastball painted the corners. His cutter worked on both sides of the plate. He didn't lean too hard on his change-up, his favorite pitch, but instead used it in particular counts. He set down the first 10 batters he faced, on just 35 pitches, and soon finished the third by stranding one of the Cardinals' four base runners in scoring position.

There was already a slim lead to protect because Yan Gomes doubled in Howie Kendrick in the second. The Nationals would leave 12 runners on base and often let Cardinals starter Miles Mikolas wiggle out of jams. Sánchez just made sure it never mattered.

The Cardinals, like the Dodgers five days ago, couldn't solve a healthy mix of his four-seam fastball, change-up, cutter and sinker. That's three

Nationals 2, Cardinals 0

WASHINGTON	AB	R	H	BI	BB	SO	AVG
Turner ss	5	0	1	0	0	1	.267
Eaton rf	5	1	1	0	0	2	.167
Rendon 3b	3	0	1	0	2	1	.348
Soto lf	5	0	1	0	0	2	.259
Kendrick 2b	4	1	2	1	1	0	.296
Zimmerman 1b	4	0	2	0	1	1	.368
Taylor cf	4	0	0	0	0	2	.250
Gomes c	3	0	2	1	1	1	.333
Sanchez p	4	0	0	0	0	2	.000
Doolittle p	0	0	0	0	0	0	---
TOTALS	37	2	10	2	5	12	—

ST. LOUIS	AB	R	H	BI	BB	SO	AVG
Fowler cf	4	0	0	0	0	1	.077
C.Martinez p	0	0	0	0	0	0	.000
Wong 2b	3	0	0	0	1	0	.217
Goldschmidt 1b	4	0	0	0	0	0	.360
Ozuna lf	4	0	0	0	0	1	.360
Molina c	2	0	0	0	0	0	.130
Carpenter 3b	3	0	0	0	0	1	.125
Edman rf	3	0	0	0	0	0	.273
DeJong ss	3	0	0	0	0	2	.190
Mikolas p	1	0	0	0	0	1	.500
Arozarena ph	0	0	0	0	0	0	.000
Gallegos p	0	0	0	0	0	0	---
Miller p	0	0	0	0	0	0	---
Brebbia p	0	0	0	0	0	0	---
Helsley p	0	0	0	0	0	0	---
J.Martinez ph	1	0	1	0	0	0	.750
Webb p	0	0	0	0	0	0	---
Bader cf	0	0	0	0	0	0	.200
TOTALS	28	0	1	0	1	6	—

WASHINGTON	010	000	100	—	2	10	1	
ST. LOUIS	000	000	000	—	0	1	0	

E: Gomes (1). **LOB:** Washington 13, St. Louis 4. **2B:** Kendrick (1), Gomes (1), Zimmerman (2). **3B:** Eaton (1). **RBI:** Gomes (1), Kendrick (6). **SB:** Arozarena (1).

WASHINGTON	IP	H	R	ER	BB	SO	NP	ERA
Sanchez	7.2	1	0	0	1	5	103	0.71
Doolittle	1.1	0	0	0	0	1	15	1.93

ST. LOUIS	IP	H	R	ER	BB	SO	NP	ERA
Mikolas	6	7	1	1	2	7	98	1.50
Gallegos	1	1	1	1	1	0	11	3.86
Miller	.1	0	0	0	0	1	7	0.00
Brebbia	1	1	0	0	1	0	18	0.00
Helsley	1	0	0	0	2	1	13	0.00
Webb	.2	1	0	0	0	1	13	3.38
C.Martinez	1	0	0	0	1	1	7	14.7

WP: Sanchez (1-0); **LP:** Mikolas (1-1); **S:** Doolittle (1). **Inherited runners-scored:** Doolittle 1-0, Miller 2-0, Brebbia 2-1, C.Martinez 1-0. **IBB:** off Mikolas (Gomes), off Gallegos (Rendon), off C.Martinez (Kendrick). **HBP:** Sanchez 2 (Arozarena,Molina). **WP:** C.Martinez. **T:** 3:24. **A:** 45,075 (45,538).

Adam Eaton dives into third base for a triple in the seventh inning. (Jonathan Newton/The Washington Post)

different fastballs coming out of the exact same arm slot. Then a change-up that looks like a fastball until, a nanosecond later, it begins falling away from swings. Coaches and teammates often praise Sánchez's ability to change speeds better than most pitchers. The Cardinals then learned that the hard way.

"He was spot on with everything today," Gomes said. "Anytime we were throwing a pitch, it meant something to set up another pitch."

The Nationals added an insurance run in the next half when Kendrick brought in Adam Eaton with a two-out single. Then Sánchez came out for the seventh while Tanner Rainey began tossing as the inning began. But Sánchez sidestepped his second hit batter, leaving Yadier Molina on first, and Rainey sat down. Sánchez was at 89 pitches and due up second in the eighth. Yet, without Hudson, Martinez needed as many outs as he could get from his starter. So he let Sánchez bat and pushed him into the eighth with the no-hitter intact.

Sánchez went this deep in about half of his starts

in the regular season. Doing so usually led to trouble. Tommy Edman hit a bullet to lead off the inning, and it seemed bound for outfield grass, but Ryan Zimmerman sprung into a dive and plucked it out of the air. Then, after Sánchez got one more hitter to fly out, José Martínez ripped a single to center, and the fans were snapped out of their hours-long lull.

"I don't claim to be superstitious," Dave Martinez said. "But when you got a no-hitter, I was freezing my butt off and didn't want to put a jacket on and I stayed with this, just this sweatshirt the whole game."

Once the hit fell, and once the short burst of noise faded, Martinez walked out to make his first and only move. Sánchez, having come so close to history, kept his head low as he walked into a high-five of teammates and out of sight. He did his job and then some. He used 103 pitches to deliver the game to the only Nationals closer in the building. And Doolittle, tasked with recording four outs, soon finished Sánchez's masterpiece by shutting the door.

Not to be overshadowed, Scherzer is lights out

Max Scherzer held the Cardinals
to one hit in seven scoreless innings.
(Jonathan Newton/The Washington Post)

By Jesse Dougherty

Max Scherzer drifted off the mound, his feet chopping into the grass, his hands ready to punch the air, while Yadier Molina's bouncer headed straight for Trea Turner's glove.

It was all Scherzer needed to polish off the best postseason start of his career. And when it went right, when the double play was turned and the seventh inning was over, Scherzer offered a quick burst of emotion before straightening up. He rolled his shoulders while turning toward the dugout. He walked in a laser-straight line and arrived there as the second Washington Nationals starter to shut down the St. Louis Cardinals in this series.

The Nationals won again Saturday, this time 3-1, after Scherzer allowed just three base runners while fanning 11.

He was only outdone by Aníbal Sánchez's $7^2/_3$ scoreless innings Friday. Both right-handers allowed a lone hit. Both rolled the Cardinals' lineup into a ball and tossed it out of sight. The Cardinals can't score, or activate their dangerous running game, if they don't have base runners.

The Nationals spent around $95 million on their rotation this season, and the investment is paying off. That's the simple way to explain their 2-0 lead in the National League Championship Series.

"I've been blessed to play behind some really, really good pitchers," right fielder Adam Eaton said. "And you just enjoy the masterpiece that they are painting."

The Nationals' pitching strategy isn't a secret. It's in the open, for everyone to see. They have six postseason wins since Oct. 1. They have needed 165 outs in those victories — counting a 10-inning defeat of the Los Angeles Dodgers in Game 5 of the NL Division Series — and all but two of them were recorded by just six pitchers: Scherzer, Stephen Strasburg, Patrick Corbin, Sánchez, Sean Doolittle and Daniel Hudson. The goal is to avoid middle relievers at all costs. The question, though, is how long can the Nationals keep this up?

They did for another day. Scherzer made sure of it. Doolittle, Corbin and Hudson notched the last six outs coming out of the bullpen. Corbin was used as a lefty-lefty specialist to face Kolten Wong in the ninth, his third relief appearance of the playoffs, and he retired him with two pitches. The Nationals did know, coming in, that this series would be different from the previous round. There are more games. There are, in turn, fewer chances to innovate.

Scherzer spent the NLDS pacing around the dugout, hands on his hips, basically begging Manager Dave Martinez for an inning out of the bullpen. The 35-year-old threw 109 pitches in Game 4, deadening his arm, and was still trying to face a batter or two when the Nationals were close to clinching. He's wired to do whatever it takes. He's also aware when situations change.

"You can't be coming out of the 'pen in the same form or fashion unless you're not going to be making your start," Scherzer said Friday afternoon, denying that he would lobby to relieve against the Cardinals. "For me, it's probably just pitch Game 2 and then wait for my next start."

So there he was about 24 hours later, stepping through the shadows of a sun-drenched afternoon, then using those shadows to dominate. Cardinals starter Adam Wainwright did the same. There was a straight line of shade cutting through the infield when Scherzer first took the mound. The hitters were in the dark, making it harder for them to read the spin of each pitch

Nationals 3, Cardinals 1

WASHINGTON	AB	R	H	BI	BB	SO	AVG
Turner ss	4	1	2	0	0	0	.294
Eaton rf	4	0	1	2	0	1	.179
Rendon 3b	3	0	1	0	1	1	.346
Soto lf	4	0	0	0	0	3	.226
Kendrick 2b	4	0	0	0	0	2	.258
Doolittle p	0	0	0	0	0	0	—
Corbin p	0	0	0	0	0	0	.000
Dan.Hudson p	0	0	0	0	0	0	—
Zimmerman 1b	4	0	0	0	0	1	.304
Suzuki c	4	0	0	0	0	3	.000
Gomes c	0	0	0	0	0	0	.333
Taylor cf	4	1	2	1	0	2	.300
Scherzer p	2	0	0	0	0	1	.000
Adams ph	1	1	1	0	0	0	.333
Dozier 2b	0	0	0	0	0	0	.000
TOTALS	34	3	7	3	1	14	—

ST. LOUIS	AB	R	H	BI	BB	SO	AVG
Fowler cf	3	0	0	0	1	2	.069
Wong 2b	3	0	0	0	0	2	.192
Goldschmidt 1b	4	0	1	0	0	2	.345
Ozuna lf	4	0	0	0	0	2	.310
Molina c	3	0	0	0	0	2	.115
Carpenter 3b	3	0	0	0	0	2	.091
Edman rf	3	0	0	0	0	2	.240
DeJong ss	3	1	1	0	0	1	.208
Wainwright p	2	0	0	0	0	1	.000
Miller p	0	0	0	0	0	0	—
J.Martinez ph	1	0	1	1	0	0	.800
Helsley p	0	0	0	0	0	0	—
TOTALS	29	1	3	1	2	12	—

```
WASHINGTON............ 001   000   020   —   3 7 0
ST. LOUIS.................. 000   000   010   —   1 3 0
```

LOB: Washington 5, St. Louis 3. **2B:** Eaton (1), J.Martinez (1). **HR:** Taylor (1), off Wainwright. **RBI:** Taylor (1), Eaton 2 (3), J.Martinez (1). **SB:** Wong (2). **GIDP:** Molina. **DP:** Washington 1 (Turner, Kendrick, Zimmerman).

WASHINGTON	IP	H	R	ER	BB	SO	NP	ERA
Scherzer	7	1	0	0	2	11	101	1.80
Doolittle	1	2	1	1	0	1	21	3.18
Corbin	0.1	0	0	0	0	0	2	7.56
Dan.Hudson	2	0	0	0	0	0	5	0.00

ST. LOUIS	IP	H	R	ER	BB	SO	NP	ERA
Wainwright	7.1	7	3	3	1	11	99	1.80
Miller	.2	0	0	0	0	1	10	0.00
Helsley	1	0	0	0	0	2	16	0.00

WP: Scherzer (2-0); **LP:** Wainwright (0-1); **S:** Dan.Hudson (3). **Inherited runners-scored:** Miller 2-0. **IBB:** off Wainwright (Rendon). **T:** 2:53. **A:** 46,458 (45,538).

Michael A. Taylor gave the Nationals their first run with a homer. (Jonathan Newton/The Washington Post)

and letting Scherzer exploit that with a mix of fastballs, change-ups and breaking balls.

He had a no-hitter until Paul Goldschmidt poked a leadoff single in the seventh. Juan Soto thought it was too low to dive for and didn't want to make an error in a one-run game. Washington got that slim lead after Michael A. Taylor hit a solo shot off Wainwright in the third.

Scherzer agreed with Soto's calculated caution, even with history on the line, because the Nationals are chasing much more than personal gain.

"Just throwing up zeros. It's a 1-0 game, mistakes are … it's razor thin out there. You can't give," Scherzer said of what was going through his mind in the seventh inning. "I'm really thinking, 'Don't give up a solo shot.'"

This all came after Sánchez carried a no-hitter for $7^2/_3$ innings Friday night. In 2013, when they were with the Detroit Tigers, Scherzer and Sánchez became the first pitchers in postseason history to hold the same team hitless through five innings of consecutive games.

Then they did it again six autumns later.

Scherzer then stranded Goldschmidt and, just two batters later, finished a 101-pitch effort with that double play.

Doolittle began warming in the bullpen as Scherzer skipped down the dugout steps. Matt Adams pinch-hit for Scherzer and pulled a single off the wall. Turner blooped a hit, and, with Wainwright nearing 100 pitches, Eaton slapped a double down the right field line.

The insurance runs helped cover a defensive mistake by Taylor in the eighth. He misjudged a liner, and, when it sneaked over his head, the Cardinals had their first and only run of the series.

But it led to nothing more. Scherzer's gem held up. And by day's end, with the sun fading against this stadium for maybe the final time this season, there was just one way to view what happened here: The Nationals marched into St. Louis, and their rotation dominated. Their starters deflated the town.

Strasburg gem puts Nats on threshold

Fans cheer the seventh of Stephen
Strasburg's 12 strikeouts.
(John McDonnell/The Washington Post)

By Thomas Boswell

Some crowd roars in sports are different. Especially if those roars have been on hold for 86 years.

The explosion in Nationals Park on Monday night as Howie Kendrick's line drive smacked off the right field scoreboard, scoring two runs and putting the Washington Nationals ahead of the St. Louis Cardinals 4-0 in the third inning of Game 3 of the National League Championship Series, was like nothing heard in a ballpark in D.C. since the Great Depression. Except that this time, the cheer was part of a nightlong Great Elation as the Nationals drubbed the Cardinals, 8-1.

A sellout crowd can't spontaneously yell words in unison without scripting. Souls, even baseball-loving souls, are not that tightly connected. But if a crowd of such size could articulate, with perfect diction and in unison, its deepest desire suddenly turned into a firm belief, those words would've been, "It's finally going to happen!"

"It," of course, has not happened yet — the return of a Washington baseball team to the World Series for the first time since 1933.

But the Nationals now lead this best-of-seven NLCS, 3-0. So far, St. Louis has been squashed flatter than a stack of 25 Cards. One more win is required to visit the World Series for the fourth time in Washington history, joining 1933, 1925 and 1924.

However, this old game has been holding postseason tournaments since 1903, and this is the number of times that a team trailing 3-0 in a seven-game series has come back to win: one.

So many people have waited so long for this. I don't even think owner Ted Lerner remembers the 1933 World Series — he was only 8.

"He always talks about going to the 1937 All-Star Game at Griffith Stadium as an early memory," said principal owner Mark Lerner, Ted's son. "[Tuesday] is my father's 94th birthday. I want it so bad for my dad. It'd bring us all to tears."

And cheers.

"The fans have definitely showed up," all-star third baseman Anthony Rendon said. "Hey, standing room only — let 'em in. The more the merrier."

This night had the feeling of a three-hour celebration more than a competition. The Nats beat not only the Cardinals but their ace, Jack Flaherty, the pitcher with the best ERA in the NL in the second half of the season: 0.94. The Nats moved that decimal point one space, up to 9.00 for the night, with four runs in just four innings.

All night, the crowd, often standing on two-strike counts, implored pitcher Stephen Strasburg, a symbol of Nats power himself, to ring up another strikeout. He obliged, fanning 12 in seven innings without yielding an earned run.

However, it was the eruptions for Nats runs that had a visceral, utterly uninhibited, doubt-free sense of release like nothing before in the 15 years since big league ball returned to Washington. This is not the teams of 2012, 2014, 2016 or 2017 that, despite 95 to 98 wins, found ways to not get past the division series. This is the team that has already won three elimination games this October — over Milwaukee in the wild-card game and in Games 4 and 5 to shock the Los Angeles Dodgers, a team most believed to be far superior.

"We've been playing pressure games for months," said Rendon, who's hitting .379 in this postseason with an 1.109 on-base-plus-slugging percentage. "We just want to ride the wave as long as we can."

In the fifth inning Monday, just as he had in the fourth, Kendrick rifled an identical-trajectory petrified rope of a double — this time off the left-

Nationals 8, Cardinals 1

ST. LOUIS	AB	R	H	BI	BB	SO	AVG
Fowler cf	4	0	0	0	0	3	.061
Wong 2b	4	0	0	0	0	0	.167
Goldschmidt 1b	4	0	0	0	0	4	.303
Ozuna lf	4	0	2	0	0	2	.333
J.Martinez rf	4	1	2	0	0	1	.667
Molina c	4	0	1	0	0	1	.133
Edman 3b	4	0	0	0	0	2	.207
DeJong ss	3	0	2	0	0	0	.259
Flaherty p	1	0	0	0	0	1	.000
Carpenter ph	1	0	0	0	0	1	.083
Webb p	0	0	0	0	0	0	—
Brebbia p	0	0	0	0	0	0	—
G.Cabrera p	0	0	0	0	0	0	—
Wieters ph	1	0	0	0	0	1	.000
Ponce de Leon p	0	0	0	0	0	0	—
TOTALS	**34**	**1**	**7**	**0**	**0**	**16**	**—**

WASHINGTON	AB	R	H	BI	BB	SO	AVG
Turner ss	4	0	0	0	0	0	.263
Eaton rf	5	1	1	1	0	1	.182
Rendon 3b	3	2	2	1	1	1	.379
Soto lf	3	1	0	0	1	2	.206
Kendrick 2b	4	2	3	3	0	1	.314
Rodney p	0	0	0	0	0	0	—
Rainey p	0	0	0	0	0	0	—
Zimmerman 1b	4	0	2	2	0	0	.333
Suzuki c	4	0	1	0	0	1	.050
Robles cf	4	2	2	1	0	1	.333
Strasburg p	1	0	0	0	0	1	.000
Dozier 2b	1	0	0	0	0	0	.000
TOTALS	**33**	**8**	**11**	**8**	**3**	**11**	**—**

ST. LOUIS	000	000	100	—	1	7	0
WASH.	004	021	10X	—	8	11	1

E: Soto (1). **LOB:** St. Louis 6, Washington 6.
2B: Ozuna (4), Rendon (4), Kendrick 3 (4), Zimmerman (3). **HR:** Robles (1), off Brebbia. **RBI:** Eaton (4), Rendon (6), Kendrick 3 (9), Zimmerman 2 (5), Robles (1).
S: Strasburg 2.

ST. LOUIS	IP	H	R	ER	BB	SO	NP	ERA
Flaherty	4	5	4	4	2	6	78	4.24
Webb	2	1	1	1	0	0	11	5.40
Brebbia	2	3	2	2	0	1	15	6.00
G.Cabrera	2	0	0	0	0	0	3	0.00
Ponce de Leon	2	2	1	1	1	4	49	4.50

WASHINGTON	IP	H	R	ER	BB	SO	NP	ERA
Strasburg	7	7	1	0	0	12	117	1.64
Rodney	1	0	0	0	0	2	13	0.00
Rainey	1	0	0	0	0	2	18	6.00

WP: Strasburg (3-0); **LP:** Flaherty (1-2).
Inherited runners-scored: Brebbia 1-1. **WP:** Flaherty.
T: 3:26. **A:** 43,675 (41,313).

Anthony Rendon, diving for a ball in the second inning, scored two runs in Game 3. (Jonathan Newton/The Washington Post)

center field wall — to drive in Rendon, who had a single, double and walk. Next, Ryan Zimmerman, the dignified old soldier of the bunch, drilled another double to score Kendrick for a 6-0 lead.

Victor Robles homered in the sixth for a 7-0 lead that sounded tantamount to a forfeit with Strasburg on the mound. The blast got the whole place standing — a posture the fans seldom abandoned for the rest of the evening.

If this night had a symbolic moment — not just for the present, but for the future — it came in the seventh inning. The Cardinals, on three singles and an outfield slip for an error by Juan Soto, finally scored a run off Strasburg. Manager Dave Martinez came to the mound.

"You grabbed your hamstring," Martinez said.

"No, I cramped up. I want to stay," Strasburg replied.

"But," Martinez said.

"I'm … in … the … game," Strasburg said.

"Let him finish [the inning]," catcher Kurt Suzuki said.

"Okay," Martinez said.

Strasburg struck out the next two Cardinals, Nos. 11 and 12. His career postseason ERA is now back to 1.10

after allowing no earned runs in seven innings.

For the final memory of a night that sets the stage for unexpected glory, perhaps soon, for a team that was left for dead in late May, just recall the greeting for Strasburg as he returned to the dugout after his 12th and final strikeout.

Gerardo (Baby Shark) Parra, Aníbal Sánchez and Max Scherzer cornered him — as teammates also did after his final regular season game — and encircled him in the kind of group hug that, in earlier years, might have embarrassed the self-contained Strasburg in the extreme.

"Not much of a hugger," Strasburg grinned afterward. "But they surrounded me."

This time — again — he seemed to love it. Why wouldn't he? After all, on Monday night, all 25 Nats, their coaches and manager, General Manager Mike Rizzo, anybody associated with this Stay in the Fight team, was encircled and trapped in an enormous hug — from 43,675 in attendance and hundreds of thousands more who would have if only their arms could stretch for miles.

One more win, never an easy one to get, and there will be champagne and citywide offers of appreciative kisses, too.

Sweep gives D.C. first pennant since 1933

The Nationals celebrate a series-clinching win in Game 4 of the NLCS. (Jonathan Newton / The Washington Post)

By Jesse Dougherty

After 86 years, after losing a baseball team for decades, then getting it back, then wondering if it would ever win the big game — or ever stop breaking hearts — the city had one more wait.

It had to wait for a finish that seemed predetermined when the Washington Nationals stepped on the field Tuesday night. It had to wait because, in this sport, there's nothing more dangerous than assumption. The Nationals were going to the World Series. That felt clear once they scored seven runs in a first inning that left little doubt. It felt clear long before the Nationals beat the St. Louis Cardinals, 7-4, to complete a four-game sweep in a National League Championship Series that was one-sided from the start. It felt a little less clear after Patrick Corbin wilted, giving four runs back, but the bullpen held strong, navigated the last 12 outs and, with that, turned waiting into sheer delirium.

Because it wasn't until the contest was over — really, really over — that the Nationals could claim Washington's first pennant since 1933. And when they did, when history collided with fate, when nothing could stand between them and the promise of a chance, they sprinted onto the field in celebration. They smiled through screams. Their relievers ran in from the bullpen, and gloves were thrown into the cool fall air, and fireworks smoke hung over a moment that was elusive no more.

"I can't put this into words," said Manager Dave Martinez, standing on a stage over second base, surrounded by ownership and the front office and the players who made this possible. Then Martinez reached for something his mother always told him. "I'll say this: Often bumpy roads lead to beautiful places. And this is a beautiful place."

That triggered one of the biggest cheers of the night. The Nationals will soon play either the Houston Astros or the New York Yankees for the title. They'll arrive there having slipped to 19-31 in mid-May, surged through the final four months of a once-lost season and collected themselves for two dances with death in the earlier rounds. First, there was Juan Soto slapping a three-run single to oust the Milwaukee Brewers in the NL wild-card game. Then there were Anthony Rendon and Soto hitting back-to-back homers off Clayton Kershaw, on back-to-back pitches, before Howie Kendrick's grand slam buried the Dodgers in Los Angeles. Next there were the Cardinals, a team that stood no chance, who were only in the way of a bulldozer without brakes.

Then came the fourth champagne celebration in the past three weeks.

"It's kind of tough to say what's going to happen in the playoffs," said Nationals pitcher Stephen Strasburg, Budweiser dripping off his beard, a smile planted on his face. "You have a great year, and you can run into a buzz saw. Maybe this year we're the buzz saw."

They have been to this point. They buried the Cardinals by scoring seven runs in the bottom of the first Tuesday night. Corbin became the first pitcher to strike out 10 in the first four innings of a postseason game. It took the Cardinals $25^2/_3$ innings to score a run off a Nationals starter in the series. St. Louis nudged back into Game 4 and had a faint pulse, but Washington's bullpen handled the rest. The chain was Tanner Rainey to Sean Doolittle to Daniel Hudson, the team's unwilling closer, who notched the final out and tossed his mitt toward the sky. He planned the celebration, modeling Doolittle's from the NL Division Series, and soon they were hugging friends and family on the field.

Most of the crowd stayed, close to 44,000 on their feet, craning their necks, lifting their cellphones, storing images for forever. They screamed themselves hoarse when the Nationals ducked into the dugout and out of sight, one after another, ready to grab a bottle and start spraying their clubhouse once again. They chugged light beer. They poured it on each other's heads. They danced to

Nationals 7, Cardinals 4

ST. LOUIS	AB	R	H	BI	BB	SO	AVG
Edman 3b-cf	4	0	0	1	1	1	.182
J.Martinez rf	4	0	1	2	0	1	.538
Goldschmidt 1b	4	0	0	0	0	3	.270
Ozuna lf	4	0	1	0	0	3	.324
Molina c	3	1	1	1	0	0	.152
DeJong ss	3	0	0	0	1	3	.233
Bader cf	2	1	0	0	1	1	.167
Carpenter ph-3b	1	0	0	0	0	0	.077
Wong 2b	4	1	2	0	0	0	.206
Dak.Hudson p	0	0	0	0	0	0	.000
Wainwright p	0	0	0	0	0	0	.000
Arozarena ph	1	0	0	0	0	1	.000
Helsley p	0	0	0	0	0	0	—
Fowler ph	0	1	0	0	1	0	.061
Gallegos p	0	0	0	0	0	0	—
Munoz ph	1	0	0	0	0	1	.000
Miller p	0	0	0	0	0	0	—
Wieters ph	1	0	0	0	0	0	.000
TOTALS	32	4	5	4	4	14	—

WASHINGTON	AB	R	H	BI	BB	SO	AVG
Turner ss	4	1	2	2	0	1	.286
Eaton rf	3	1	1	0	1	0	.194
Rendon 3b	3	0	1	1	0	0	.375
Soto lf	4	1	2	1	0	0	.237
Kendrick 2b	3	1	0	0	1	1	.289
Dan.Hudson p	0	0	0	0	0	0	—
Zimmerman 1b	4	1	0	0	0	1	.290
Robles cf	4	1	1	1	0	1	.313
Gomes c	4	1	1	2	0	2	.308
Corbin p	1	0	0	0	0	1	.000
Rainey p	0	0	0	0	0	0	—
Parra ph	1	0	1	0	0	0	.333
Doolittle p	0	0	0	0	0	0	—
Dozier 2b	0	0	0	0	0	0	.000
TOTALS	31	7	9	7	2	7	—

ST. LOUIS	000	130	000	—	4	5	1
WASHINGTON	700	000	00X	—	7	9	0

E: Wong (2). **LOB:** St. Louis 6, Washington 4.
2B: J.Martinez (2), Eaton (2), Soto (1). **HR:** Molina (1), off Corbin. **RBI:** Molina (3), Edman (3), J.Martinez 2 (3), Rendon (7), Soto (7), Robles (2), Gomes 2 (3), Turner 2 (3). **SF:** Rendon. **S:** Corbin.
DP: St. Louis 1 (Edman, Wong, Goldschmidt).

ST. LOUIS	IP	H	R	ER	BB	SO	NP	ERA
Dak.Hudson	1	5	7	4	1	0	15	9.00
Wainwright	1.2	2	0	0	0	0	16	1.62
Helsley	2	0	0	0	1	1	27	0.00
Gallegos	2	1	0	0	0	3	20	2.08
Miller	2	1	0	0	0	3	29	0.00

WASHINGTON	IP	H	R	ER	BB	SO	NP	ERA
Corbin	5	4	4	4	3	12	94	7.43
Rainey	1	0	0	0	0	1	16	4.50
Doolittle	1.2	1	0	0	0	1	21	2.45
Dan.Hudson	1.1	0	0	0	1	0	26	0.00

WP: Corbin (1-2) **LP:** Dak.Hudson (0-1)
S: Dan.Hudson (4).
Inherited runners-scored: Wainwright 2-2, Dan.Hudson 1-0. **IBB:** off Dak.Hudson (Kendrick). **HBP:** Dan.Hudson (Molina).
T: 3:02. **A:** 43,976 (41,313).

From left, Howie Kendrick, Trea Turner (in helmet), Aníbal Sánchez and Brian Dozier (with trophy). (Toni L. Sandys/The Washington Post)

all kinds of music — Mexican pop, rap, even slow country — and that's when Max Scherzer stumbled into a quiet part of the room.

Scherzer, the team's ace, its backbone, the pitcher who has lifted them to so many heights, drifted off by himself. He hopped up and down. He couldn't stop grinning. Then he walked up to a row of plastic-lined lockers, stared right into them and cried. They came and went, those tears, but they'd been suppressed by years of missed opportunity. He quickly wiped his red face, drops of alcohol flying off it, and did a light jog back in the mix. There was a team to party with. And, whenever it dissipated, there'd be one more to chase.

"It took the entire roster," Scherzer said. "Everyone on the roster had a hand in it."

This all began back in early February, in West Palm Beach, Fla., on a cool morning that signaled the return of familiar routine. That was 245 days ago. Martinez stood by his office and sipped coffee from a foam cup. Scherzer charged toward the batting cages with a fresh helmet pushed onto his head. And there those two words — World Series — blended into quiet conversations, bent into a new shape once superstar Bryce Harper departed for

Philadelphia. They're now a constant in Washington, at least in spring, when hope floats higher than the beating sun. This season was no different. It began with dreams.

Yet they were dimmed, considerably, by a start that put the Nationals on life support. Martinez's job was in jeopardy. There seemed to be good, logical reasons to trade cornerstone veterans. There was no reason to believe the remaining season, let alone autumn, would ever count. But Martinez didn't panic. Neither did the team around him. Mark Lerner, the managing principal owner, says now that he never considered firing Martinez. He didn't know if the season would turn around — he even admits wondering how it could — but trusted the coaches and players to try. Trust is a common word around here. So they turned a final chance into a whole lot more.

They first woke up on the doorstep of summer. Then they went into overdrive, going on the best 80-game stretch in club history, later tossing the Brewers and Dodgers off their postseason path. Then there they were Tuesday night, bashing the Cardinals one last time, earning baseball's right to play on.

Only two teams get a shot in the World Series each October. The Washington Nationals will be one of them.

Isn't it grand?

Nationals second baseman Howie Kendrick yells at the dugout after hitting the series-winning grand slam in the 10th inning of Game 5. (John McDonnell/The Washington Post)

By Barry Svrluga

In some way, this entire season was about how it started and how they responded. The Washington Nationals were 19-31 on May 23, dead and done — then played the rest of the season on a 107-win pace to make the postseason. They were down two runs with four outs to give in the National League wild-card game — and won.

And here they were Wednesday night, somehow in a tempest in Southern California. The Los Angeles Dodgers had milked 117 pitches from their star on the rise, right-hander Walker Buehler. The Nats had mostly flailed. They trailed by two runs. They had six outs remaining. And they faced the generational left-hander, Clayton Kershaw.

Anthony Rendon, Juan Soto, Howie Kendrick — ready for your capes?

"This team, man," Max Scherzer said. "This team."

We're in new territory, Washington, because the Nats on Wednesday night embodied the Nats in 2019, and they have now busted open this postseason with a mind-bending 7-3 victory in Game 5 of their NL Division Series that wasn't decided until Kendrick's grand slam in the top of the 10th.

Finally, someone else felt the heat. For once, the Nats forced a fold, one that will be felt for years around here. And for the first time, Washington will appear in a NL Championship Series because of all of it — performance, for sure, but personality and perseverance, too. The situation — in the season, or in a game — didn't matter. The Nats entered the sixth inning Wednesday trailing 3-0, entered the eighth trailing 3-1 — and won going away.

"A lot of teams would have folded," General Manager Mike Rizzo said. "A lot of teams would have pointed fingers. This team is resilient."

Nationally, the result will hang on Kershaw, because as great as he is (or was), he failed — and epically — in the postseason again. The Dodgers' World Series drought now reaches 31 years, and that one fact will haunt Kershaw through the holidays. Dodgers Manager Dave Roberts might not enjoy his eggnog given he set up the legend to fail, and he was booed roundly by a rapidly exiting Dodger Stadium crowd when he appeared on the field in the 10th. Yet it's on Kershaw, a tragic figure.

But in the District, why not make this about heroes rather than goats? That's what, for the first time in a postseason history riddled with gut punches and gray hairs, we have now.

Oh, and make it about ghosts, too. Because they've suddenly vanished.

"We've been battling so many years to be able to push through," Scherzer said in a raucous and sopping visitors' clubhouse. "And we've been in some tough, tough losses. To finally come through with a huge win, man. Man. I can't. … That's it."

The emotions are hard to describe. The heroes aren't. Get to them pronto.

We have Rendon, the Nats' best player, with a double to start the Nationals' first rally in the sixth, then an absolute blast off Kershaw to open the eighth, pulling them within a run, creating hope in the first base dugout and doubt on the third base side. That would have been enough. But Tony Two-Bags added one more pure stroke, a double to put runners on second and third in the 10th.

We have Soto, the wunderkind who struts, of all things, his takes, and finally admitted Wednesday he does it to rattle opposing pitchers. The thing about his eighth-inning at-bat against Kershaw, already wounded by Rendon: Soto didn't have a take about which to strut. Instead, he welcomed the only pitch he saw, an 89-mph slider, into his kitchen and immediately sent it back from whence it came, a missile out to right-center. One more nugget: Soto is so dangerous that Roberts ordered him intentionally walked by Joe Kelly to load the bases in that fateful 10th.

And we have Kendrick, once a Dodger, in the lineup because of his bat despite his questionable defense. These were the first contending Nats without Bryce Harper, the departed free agent who left them not only with less star power but without a key left-handed bat. And yet, Roberts froze when tasked with navigating Rendon-to-Soto-to-Kendrick, right-to-left-to-right.

"That's the gantlet that teams have to run through," Rizzo said. "When we go our top five, six hitters, we're as good as anybody. And in those situations, I feel good that they're going to make something happen."

When Kendrick came up to face Kelly, he had contributed the following: an error, two strikeouts, a grounder that turned into a double play and a flyball on which Dodgers center fielder Cody Bellinger made an acrobatic catch. But the acceptable results here included a squibber off the end of the bat that found a hole. Or a medium-deep flyball that could score Adam Eaton from third.

He fouled off a curveball but had a notion. The 0-1 pitch would be heat.

"I was sitting fastball," Kendrick said.

What moments, in the relatively brief history of this franchise's existence in the District, stand out? There will always be something about Liván Hernández on the mound at RFK Stadium, because baseball returned in April 2005 after a three-decade drought. Ryan Zimmerman christened the new yard with a walk-off homer on national television three years later, but that team lost 100 games. Harper wrapped his head in a District flag and won the Home Run Derby last summer, but that was an exhibition, and then Bryce bolted.

For years, the best postseason memory to which the Nats could point was Jayson Werth's walk-off homer in Game 4 of the 2012 Division Series against St. Louis. It was an indelible moment. But in the end, the series was lost in a manner that will make you double over still.

Nice moment. Didn't matter. Ultimately, it didn't matter.

Now, though, we have Kendrick turning around 97 mph from Kelly. Grand slam. Ballgame.

"You couldn't dream of something like that," Kendrick said.

When are those flights to St. Louis? The Nats now have their moments that matter.

They also have more baseball to play, and because of that, we can further buy in to who they are. Five years ago, when the underdog San Francisco Giants won the wild-card game to win the right to take on the best-in-the-NL Nats, veteran pitcher Tim Hudson asked the question that would define the series: "What do you have between your legs?"

These Nats have, um, a spine — and more. Baby Shark. Stay in the Fight. Go 1-0 today. Home run dances. Gimmicks? Fine. Don't go questioning them now, because we have evidence — hard-earned evidence — of the results.

Kurt Suzuki completing a seven-run, ninth-inning comeback against the Mets. Stephen Strasburg coming out of the bullpen against the Brewers. Soto with the hit that won that game. Scherzer out of the 'pen in Game 2 to strike out the side. Zim with the three-run bomb and Max with an empty-the-tank 109 pitches in Game 4, forcing the flight here.

And now, Howie Kendrick against Joe Kelly.

There were more heroes Wednesday night. There could be more heroes still. What's important: This game had a different flavor. This team has a different flavor. So it's fair to say the end will have a different flavor. You could have said that had they lost Wednesday night. But they didn't. They won.

Let's see what that tastes like for another week — or more.

Fifth-inning error proves costly in series opener

By Jesse Dougherty

If Howie Kendrick plants his glove on the dirt, if his reaction is just a twitch or two quicker, if he does anything to keep that rocketed baseball in front of him, then maybe the final innings unfold a little bit differently for the Washington Nationals.

But Kendrick's mitt didn't get there in time. Instead, in the fifth inning, in one of the biggest moments of Game 1 of the National League Division Series, a 96-mph grounder slipped through his legs and into right field to gift the Los Angeles Dodgers a precious second run Thursday night. Washington eventually fell to the Dodgers, 6-0, in a defeat that had all the makings of a missed opportunity.

"We didn't play very well today," Manager Dave Martinez said, putting it bluntly, passing the blame around to both his offense and pitching staff. "Walked a lot of guys. Chased a lot of bad pitches."

The Nationals got a gutsy outing from Patrick Corbin despite a shaky first and despite the many jams he navigated in six innings. But strong starting pitching needs to be complemented. It can't win games by itself. Washington instead got shoddy defense from Kendrick, their 36-year-old first baseman, and managed just two hits against Walker Buehler and the Dodgers' bullpen.

Kendrick finished with two errors and could have been charged with a third. The fifth-inning miscue doubled a one-run deficit, and after Fernando Rodney allowed two more in the seventh, the Nationals had buried themselves. Then Hunter Strickland allowed two solo homers in the eighth to make it seem as if Corbin never pitched in the first place.

"Pat, I feel bad for Pat," Kendrick said. "He threw a heck of game, too. A couple mistakes on my behalf out there. It's part of the game. But you never want to let your teammates down."

This goes back to Dec. 4, 2018, to the first days of a busy offseason, to when the Nationals signed Corbin to a six-year deal worth $140 million. The move added Corbin to a rotation already headlined by Max Scherzer and Stephen Strasburg. It strengthened Washington's years-long commitment to building a contender through starting pitching. And it soon became one of the three reasons the Nationals always believed they could excel in this exact playoff matchup.

They just had to get here. They just had to stare down a season-ending defeat, with four outs to go against the Milwaukee Brewers in the wild-card game, and have 20-year-old Juan Soto lift them onto a plane to Los Angeles. Soto's single is what pushed the Nationals deeper into October, for at least a few more days, for a chance to knock off the 106-win Dodgers. Then the rotation grabbed the torch.

But Corbin's first postseason appearance didn't begin how he wanted. Kendrick and the bullpen later made sure it wouldn't end how Corbin wanted, either. Corbin walked four batters because he couldn't locate his

Dodgers 6, Nationals 0

WASHINGTON	AB	R	H	BI	BB	SO	AVG
T.Turner ss	4	0	1	0	0	1	.250
Eaton rf	3	0	0	0	1	1	.000
Rendon 3b	3	0	0	0	1	2	.000
Soto lf	4	0	1	0	0	2	.250
Kendrick 1b	2	0	0	0	1	1	.200
Cabrera 2b	3	0	0	0	0	0	.000
Robles cf	3	0	0	0	0	1	.167
Gomes c	3	0	0	0	0	3	.000
Corbin p	2	0	0	0	0	2	.000
Rainey p	0	0	0	0	0	0	---
Rodney p	0	0	0	0	0	0	---
Parra ph	1	0	0	0	0	0	.000
Strickland p	0	0	0	0	0	0	---
TOTALS	28	0	2	0	3	13	—

L.A.	AB	R	H	BI	BB	SO	AVG
Pollock lf	4	1	0	0	1	3	.000
Kelly p	0	0	0	0	0	0	---
Freese 1b	3	0	0	0	0	2	.000
Pederson ph-rf	1	2	1	1	1	0	1.00
J.Turner 3b	5	1	1	0	0	2	.200
Bellinger cf-1b-cf	2	1	0	0	2	2	.000
C.Taylor rf-cf-lf	2	0	1	0	2	0	.500
Muncy 2b-1b	3	0	2	3	1	0	.667
Seager ss	4	0	1	0	0	0	.250
Smith c	4	0	0	0	0	2	.000
Buehler p	2	0	0	0	0	1	.000
Hernandez ph	1	0	0	0	0	0	.000
Kolarek p	0	0	0	0	0	0	---
Maeda p	0	0	0	0	0	0	---
Lux ph-2b	1	1	1	1	0	0	1.00
TOTALS	32	6	7	5	7	12	—

WASHINGTON	000	000	000	—	0	2	2
L.A.	100	010	22X	—	6	7	0

E: Kendrick 2 (2). **LOB:** Washington 4, Los Angeles 9.
2B: T.Turner (1). **HR:** Lux (1), off Strickland; Pederson (1), off Strickland. **RBI:** Muncy 3 (3), Lux (1), Pederson (1). **SB:** J.Turner (1), Muncy (1).
DP: Los Angeles 1 (J.Turner, Freese, J.Turner).

WASHINGTON	IP	H	R	ER	BB	SO	NP	ERA
Corbin	6	3	2	1	5	9	107	1.50
Rainey	1	1	2	2	1	1	16	54.0
Rodney	.2	1	0	0	1	1	23	0.00
Strickland	1	2	2	2	0	1	27	18.0

L.A.	IP	H	R	ER	BB	SO	NP	ERA
Buehler	6	1	0	0	3	8	100	0.00
Kolarek	0.1	0	0	0	1	0	3	0.00
Maeda	1.2	0	0	0	0	2	19	0.00
Kelly	1	1	0	0	0	2	16	0.00

WP: Buehler (1-0); **LP:** Corbin (0-1).
Inherited runners-scored: Rodney 2-2. **PB:** Gomes (1).
T: 3:23. **A:** 53,095 (56,000).

From left, Fernando Rodney, Wander Suero and Austin Voth during the introduction ceremony. (John McDonnell/The Washington Post)

slider in the first. The Dodgers, in turn, took an early lead without putting the ball in play. He got up to 31 pitches, a yawning first-inning total, yet limited the damage to one run by getting a grounder to first. The slow start was dangerous in one very clear way: Washington arrived in the postseason despite having the National League's worst bullpen. Now it needed Corbin to go as deep as he could.

And while he did, working a one-two-three third, then wiggling out of trouble in the fourth, Buehler's pitch count climbed even faster. The Dodgers' starter issued three walks in the fourth but kept the Nationals off the scoreboard. He finished that inning at 76 pitches, outpacing Corbin for who would get hooked first, and that gave Washington a chance at challenging some of the Dodgers' relievers.

But before that happened, before any reliever appeared, Kendrick's second error let the Dodgers inch further ahead. His first one was inconsequential, on a Buehler grounder in the second inning, only costing Corbin few extra pitches as he settled in. The second one cost the Nationals a run and cast doubt over whether Kendrick should play first again in Game 2 on Friday.

"That's going to happen in this game. Unfortunately it's in the postseason," Kendrick said of the error in the fifth. "But I wouldn't change anything about how I tried to make that play."

Kendrick has so often paced the Nationals with his bat this season. He hit .344 and posted the league's best batting average in September. His defense was rock solid until he slipped in the second and again with two down in the fifth. He made one error in 304 chances during the regular season. He then made two in five opportunities against the Dodgers. Those were etched into the box score. A third mistake came on a Corey Seager single that whizzed beneath his glove. Ryan Zimmerman looked on from the bench. Kendrick was soon there, too, standing among teammates between innings, his brows furrowed as he stared out at the field.

Corbin soon finished the sixth at 107 pitches. He struck out nine. He allowed two runs, just one of them earned, and was imperfect in giving the Nationals a puncher's chance. But his effort wasn't matched by the Nationals in the field or at the plate or out of the bullpen. And so a fragile winning formula, thought up last winter, tried and tested throughout the season, was entirely incomplete.

Series in their hands, top arms get job done

Nationals starting pitcher Stephen Strasburg
struck out 10 in six stellar innings.
(John McDonnell/The Washington Post)

By Jesse Dougherty

There was a point inside Dodger Stadium on Friday night, right around the seventh inning, when all the math was stripped down to something very simple: The Los Angeles Dodgers were only going to face the Washington Nationals' very best pitchers. And if they couldn't beat Stephen Strasburg, Sean Doolittle, Max Scherzer and Daniel Hudson, in that order, then the Nationals would win and even this National League Division Series at a game apiece.

That what's happened once nine innings were added up. The Nationals beat the Dodgers, 4-2, because Strasburg went through their order like a wrecking ball and a makeshift bullpen held on. Strasburg retired the first 14 batters he faced. He struck out 10, just two days after throwing 34 pitches in the wild-card game, and the victory was finished off by Doolittle, Scherzer and Hudson out of the bullpen. Manager Dave Martinez left nothing to chance. He may have hooked Scherzer in time to still start him in Washington on Sunday, though that remains to be seen.

It all helped the Nationals head home with a series split in hand.

When they arrived Friday, when they took stock of their series-opening loss — just two hits, 13 strikeouts, another bullpen implosion — they could take comfort in a simple fact: It was only one game. It didn't end their season. It stung, and it wasn't pretty, and they certainly tightened up, but there was a reason to breathe a little. Strasburg's been their anchor. And, until the Dodgers scored off him in the sixth, he had not allowed a run in 23 consecutive postseason innings.

But the Nationals had immediately given him a lead to protect. They loaded the bases in the first inning before Howie Kendrick singled in Trea Turner. But then they wilted. Ryan Zimmerman popped out on a first-pitch fastball. Kurt Suzuki struck out in a full count, on Clayton Kershaw's low-and-in slider, and those at-bats could have haunted Washington later. Instead, in the next inning, the Nationals rallied for two more runs with Adam Eaton's single and Anthony Rendon's double off the left-center wall.

That gave Strasburg a three-run cushion to protect. That gave their dugout, quiet for most of Thursday evening, a reason to bang on the padded railing and pass around high-fives. The big remaining question was how far Strasburg could go and how Martinez would use his bullpen. In Game 1, the Dodgers feasted against Tanner Rainey, Fernando Rodney and Hunter Strickland. It made it clear that Martinez, who has dealt with a flaky bullpen all season, carried two big problems into these playoffs: There is a yawning gap between his rotation and trustworthy relievers. And he only has two of those in Hudson and Doolittle.

Yet first Strasburg cruised, one batter at a time, using 85 pitches to craft a work of art. He struck out two in the first. Kershaw was the first batter to hit something into the outfield, lining one to left with two outs in the third, but Juan Soto sprinted in to make a diving catch. Strasburg nodded, patting his glove with a closed fist, then bobbed his head as he disappeared down the tunnel.

It looked like there may be a slow beat playing in his head. Or maybe that's just the zone he sinks into, as if the stadium were empty, as if all he had to do was choose the pitches his opponents swing at. As if throwing 14 curveballs to the first eight batters was routine, regular, something Strasburg really did by disregarding counts and putting the entire night on his terms.

Strasburg wound up throwing 34 curveballs to a team that crushes heat.

NATIONALS 4, DODGERS 2

WASHINGTON	AB	R	H	BI	BB	SO	AVG
T.Turner ss	5	1	2	0	0	0	.308
Eaton rf	5	1	2	1	0	0	.182
Rendon 3b	4	0	2	1	1	1	.200
Soto lf	4	0	0	0	0	1	.167
Kendrick 2b	5	0	1	1	0	0	.200
Zimmerman 1b	4	1	1	0	0	1	.400
Suzuki c	3	0	0	0	1	1	.000
Robles cf	2	1	1	0	0	0	.250
M.Taylor cf	0	0	0	0	0	0	---
Strasburg p	2	0	0	0	0	1	.000
Doolittle p	0	0	0	0	0	0	---
Cabrera ph	1	0	1	1	0	0	.143
Scherzer p	0	0	0	0	0	0	.000
Hudson p	0	0	0	0	0	0	---
TOTALS	35	4	10	4	2	5	—

L.A.	AB	R	H	BI	BB	SO	AVG
Pederson rf	4	0	1	0	0	2	.400
J.Turner 3b	3	0	1	1	0	0	.250
Pollock lf	4	0	0	0	0	3	.000
Bellinger cf	4	0	0	0	0	2	.000
Muncy 1b	3	1	1	1	1	2	.500
Smith c	3	0	1	0	1	1	.143
Seager ss	4	0	0	0	0	3	.125
Lux 2b	3	0	0	0	0	3	.250
Kershaw p	1	0	0	0	0	0	.000
Beaty ph	1	1	1	0	0	0	1.00
Baez p	0	0	0	0	0	0	---
Kolarek p	0	0	0	0	0	0	---
May p	0	0	0	0	0	0	---
C.Taylor ph	1	0	0	0	0	1	.333
Urias p	0	0	0	0	0	0	---
TOTALS	31	2	5	2	2	17	—

WASHINGTON	120	000	010	—	4	10	0
L.A.	000	001	100	—	2	5	1

E: Urias (1). **LOB:** Washington 10, Los Angeles 5. **2B:** T.Turner (2), Rendon (1), Robles (1), Zimmerman (1), Pederson (1), J.Turner (1). **HR:** Muncy (1), off Doolittle. **RBI:** Kendrick (1), Eaton (1), Rendon (1), Cabrera (1), J.Turner (1), Muncy (4). **SF:** J.Turner. **S:** Strasburg, Robles.

WASHINGTON	IP	H	R	ER	BB	SO	NP	ERA
Strasburg	6	3	1	1	0	10	85	1.00
Doolittle	1	1	1	1	0	2	16	9.00
Scherzer	1	0	0	0	0	3	14	4.50
Hudson	1	1	0	0	2	2	23	0.00

L.A.	IP	H	R	ER	BB	SO	NP	ERA
Kershaw	6	6	3	3	1	4	99	4.50
Baez	1	2	0	0	0	1	12	0.00
Kolarek	1	0	0	0	0	3	9	0.00
May	1.1	2	1	1	0	0	21	6.75
Urias	1	0	0	0	0	0	18	0.00

WP: Strasburg, (2-0); **LP:** Kershaw, (0-1); **S:** Hudson, (2). **Inherited runners-scored:** Kolarek 2-0, May 2-0. **T:** 3:37. **A:** 53,086 (56,000).

Victor Robles scores in the first inning of Game 2. (John McDonnell/The Washington Post)

He threw more than ever this season, right around 30 percent of his total pitches, because his velocity is lower and his career is into its back half. But his effectiveness hasn't wavered. This only showed that it may be sloping still.

Will Smith broke up Strasburg's perfect game with two outs in the fifth. Justin Turner broke up his shutout an inning later. Then Martinez made the critical decision of bringing Doolittle in from the bullpen after Strasburg allowed two hits in the sixth. Doolittle allowed a solo homer to Max Muncy in the seventh. That shaved the Nationals' lead down to one. They restored it on Asdrúbal Cabrera's RBI single in the next half.

Then Martinez made the off-the-wall decision of plugging in Scherzer for the eighth. Martinez announced Friday afternoon that Scherzer would start Game 3 in Washington on Sunday. Now here he was in the eighth, stalking his way through the infield grass, soon striking out the side on 14 pitches that seemed allergic to wood. Scherzer shook Martinez's hand in the dugout. He more so slapped it and held on. He was finished. He paced as the rest unfolded, hands on his hips, and Hudson stranded the bases loaded in a roller-coaster ninth.

The Nationals finally chose to live or die with their small group of top arms. The result gave them a pulse.

Dodgers batter Corbin and reclaim series lead

By Jesse Dougherty

Here came Patrick Corbin, gliding across the outfield grass, the Washington Nationals' latest escape plan resting squarely on his left arm.

They needed 12 more outs against the Los Angeles Dodgers on Sunday night. They needed Corbin, the third ace of their stacked rotation, the pitcher they signed to a huge contract last winter, to get at least three of them. But he couldn't. He instead gave up a two-run double, and then he gave up another, and then the Dodgers beat the Nationals, 10-4, because everything went sideways in that sixth inning. Six runs stained Corbin's final line. That only stung more once Washington made a small push that couldn't cover the bullpen's mess. The Nationals now face elimination in Game 4 at Nationals Park on Monday.

Dave Martinez preaches "the little things." The Nationals need them more than ever.

Corbin was, in theory, brought to Washington for moments such as this. Not necessarily a relief appearance — and not necessarily a relief appearance in the guts of the National League Division Series — but for whenever the stakes were climbing. That was now.

And then now proved too much for him.

"It just stinks," Corbin said, his voice lowered a bit, his locker surrounded by two dozen reporters for the wrong reasons. "I feel like I let these guys down."

The Nationals' first critical decision arrived at the onset of this game. They could have pushed Max Scherzer to start, as previously scheduled, even after he threw 14 pitches out of the bullpen in a Game 2 victory on Friday. It was the riskier option. It also fit with Washington's willingness to do anything for an edge. But the calculations still led Scherzer and Manager Dave Martinez to restraint. Scherzer told Martinez that the Nationals would get his best after one more day of rest. Martinez agreed, and with that he shifted to 35-year-old Aníbal Sánchez.

And Sánchez was excellent until Max Muncy tagged him for a towering, two-out home run in the fifth. He otherwise struck out nine in five innings. The Nationals still had the lead when Sánchez exited, thanks to a two-run homer from Juan Soto in the first, but there were still four innings to pitch. Corbin was the first reliever to loosen. It didn't matter that he had thrown six innings and 107 pitches just three days earlier.

This was a continuation of the Nationals' insistence on hiding their middle relievers at all costs. Martinez has made it clear that he trusts six pitchers on his roster: Scherzer, Strasburg, Corbin, Sánchez and relievers Daniel Hudson and Sean Doolittle. That's it. That's why Martinez brought in Scherzer for the eighth inning of Game 2. And that's why Corbin became the latest starter to moonlight in the bullpen. It seemed conceivable, at least for a moment, that a combination of Corbin, Doolittle and Hudson could finish the game. Then the

Dodgers 10,
Nationals 4

L.A.	AB	R	H	BI	BB	SO	AVG
Pederson rf	2	0	0	0	1	1	.286
Hernandez ph-rf	2	1	1	2	1	1	.333
Muncy 1b-2b	4	2	1	1	2	0	.400
J.Turner 3b	6	1	3	3	0	0	.357
Bellinger cf	5	1	2	0	0	1	.182
Seager ss	4	0	1	0	1	1	.167
Pollock lf	3	0	0	0	0	3	.000
Kelly p	0	0	0	0	0	0	.000
Urias p	1	0	0	0	0	1	.000
Beaty ph	1	0	0	0	0	0	.500
Kolarek p	0	0	0	0	0	0	.000
Maeda p	0	0	0	0	0	0	.000
Jansen p	0	0	0	0	0	0	.000
Lux 2b	2	0	1	0	0	1	.333
Freese ph-1b	3	2	3	0	0	0	.500
Martin c	4	2	2	4	1	2	.500
Ryu p	2	0	0	0	0	2	.000
C.Taylor ph-lf	2	1	0	0	1	2	.200
TOTALS	**41**	**10**	**14**	**10**	**7**	**15**	**—**

WASHINGTON	AB	R	H	BI	BB	SO	AVG
T.Turner ss	3	0	0	0	1	0	.250
Eaton rf	3	1	1	0	1	0	.214
Rendon 3b	3	1	1	0	1	0	.231
Soto lf	3	2	2	2	1	1	.267
Kendrick 1b	4	0	1	0	0	0	.214
Suzuki c	2	0	0	0	0	1	.000
Gomes c	1	0	0	0	1	0	.000
Dozier 2b	2	0	0	0	0	1	.000
Cabrera ph-2b	1	0	0	1	0	1	.125
M.Taylor cf	4	0	1	0	0	1	.250
Sanchez p	1	0	0	0	0	1	.000
Zimmerman ph	1	0	0	0	0	0	.333
Corbin p	0	0	0	0	0	0	.000
Suero p	0	0	0	0	0	0	.000
Rodney p	0	0	0	0	0	0	.000
Parra ph	1	0	0	0	0	0	.000
Rainey p	0	0	0	0	0	0	.000
Strickland	0	0	0	0	0	0	.000
Adams ph	1	0	0	0	0	0	.000
TOTALS	**30**	**4**	**6**	**3**	**5**	**6**	**—**

L.A.	000	017	002	—	10	14	0
WASHINGTON	200	002	000	—	4	6	0

LOB: Los Angeles 11, Washington 5. **2B:** J.Turner (2), Martin (1), Hernandez (1), Bellinger (1), Freese (1). **HR:** Muncy (2), off Sanchez; J.Turner (1), off Suero; Martin (1), off Strickland; Soto (1), off Ryu. **RBI:** Muncy (5), Martin 4 (4), Hernandez 2 (2), J.Turner 3 (4), Soto 2 (4), Cabrera (2). **SF:** Cabrera. **DP:** Los Angeles 2 (J.Turner, Lux, Muncy; Freese, Hernandez, J.Turner).

L.A.	IP	H	R	ER	BB	SO	NP	ERA
Ryu	5	4	2	2	2	3	74	3.60
Kelly	0	1	2	2	3	0	22	18.0
Urias	2	1	0	0	0	0	15	0.00
Kolarek	1	0	0	0	0	1	6	0.00
Maeda	2	0	0	0	0	0	5	0.00
Jansen	1	0	0	0	0	2	9	0.00

WASHINGTON	IP	H	R	ER	BB	SO	NP	ERA
Sanchez	5	4	1	1	2	9	87	1.80
Corbin	.2	4	6	6	2	2	35	9.45
Suero	.1	2	1	1	0	0	13	27.0
Rodney	1	1	0	0	2	2	31	0.00
Rainey	1	1	0	0	0	0	13	13.5
Strickland	1	2	2	2	1	2	28	18.0

WP: Ryu (1-0); **LP:** Corbin (0-2). Kelly pitched to 4 batters in the 6th **Inherited runners-scored:** Urias 3-1, Suero 2-2. **IBB:** off Ryu (T.Turner), off Corbin (Muncy). **WP:** Kelly, Rodney, Rainey. **T:** 3:58. **A:** 43,423 (41,313).

Patrick Corbin gave up six runs in two-thirds of an inning in relief. (John McDonnell/The Washington Post)

experiment disintegrated in Corbin's hands.

The meat of the Dodgers' order was waiting for Corbin. His slider was off. He issued a leadoff single to Cody Bellinger, who had been hitless in the series, before settling the danger with back-to-back strikeouts. He just couldn't find his way out of the woods.

"You don't have that time to set your pitches up going into it," catcher Yan Gomes said of Corbin making a relief appearance instead of starting. "They already knew what we were going with, and they had some really good at-bats against us."

Dodgers Manager Dave Roberts had set up his lineup with the thought of Corbin entering at some point. Roberts was fine with pinch-hitting for two of his lefties — there were five in his original order — starting when he lifted Gavin Lux for David Freese. Freese dribbled a single through the right side of the infield. That brought up Russell Martin, who hit .220 this season, and he rocked a low slider into the left-center gap.

Then Corbin lost control. He walked Chris Taylor with four erratic pitches. He let Enrique Hernández stretch the lead with a second two-run double that restarted the carousel around the bases. Hernández was pinch-hitting for the left-handed Joc Pederson. The rally put the Dodgers' depth on full display. The doubles came on Corbin's slider, his best pitch but a pitch that didn't have

its usual break when he most needed it to.

His final act of the night was standing on the mound while the Nationals intentionally walked Muncy. He then exited the field. The crowd quieted around him after 35 fateful pitches, and that's when Justin Turner launched a three-run homer off Wander Suero. All seven of the Dodgers' sixth-inning runs came with two outs and two strikes. That's how slim the Nationals' margin for error was. That's what separates winners from losers in October.

"We were at a good spot in the lineup where we thought Corbin could get through it," Martinez said. "And his stuff was good. ... He had every hitter 0-2. He just couldn't finish."

They turned to Corbin — and Scherzer two nights earlier — to avoid using any of Suero, Fernando Rodney, Hunter Strickland or Tanner Rainey in big spots. Strickland later gave up a two-run homer to Martin in the ninth. That was the ninth homer he has allowed in 13 career postseason innings. That was more evidence of why there was such an outsize effort to hide them in the first place. But it was too late for the Nationals to reverse course. They tried to use Corbin as a Band-Aid. It didn't work. They will now need a new plan Monday, facing elimination, figuring it will be Scherzer until he has absolutely nothing left.

Zimmerman blast gives Nats golden opportunity

First base coach Tim Bogar is every bit as fired up as the Nationals Park crowd about Ryan Zimmerman's three-run homer in the fifth inning. (Jonathan Newton/The Washington Post)

By Thomas Boswell

Moments such as Ryan Zimmerman's 10-minute-goose-bump home run at Nationals Park on Monday night in Game 4 of the National League Division Series are why baseball is played and why we watch it for a lifetime.

The oft-injured Zimmerman, 35, has been unseen for months at a time this season. Years removed from his turn as Face of the Franchise, he has been consigned by many to the sport's scrap heap. But in the fifth inning, with the Nats clinging to a 2-1 lead in an elimination game against the august Los Angeles Dodgers, Zimmerman blasted a monstrously high flyball that momentarily disappeared from sight at light-tower level. The drive seemed to hang, blocked and battered by a flag-snapping crosswind from left to right field that should have knocked it down into a fielder's glove.

But when Zimmerman's three-run blast landed well onto the center field batter's-eye grass, it was the Dodgers who were knocked to the deck, trailing 5-1 and on the way to a 6-1 loss that forced a decisive Game 5 in Los Angeles.

Asked after his heroics about the chance that this might have been the last game he ever plays in Nationals Park, he began to repeat his pregame quote on the same subject: "I plan on playing more games. I feel like a lot of people think I'm not going to play more games [ever again]. But I feel good. I feel like . . ."

Max Scherzer, sitting on the postgame interview podium, cut Zim off, snapping sarcastically: "I really don't think these are his last games. Only you think these are his last games."

Talk about a contract push!

Let the record show that, after a fist pump at first base, Zimmerman ran the bases with hard determination still locked on his face — perhaps showing how desperately he felt the need to deliver after striking out in his first two at-bats. The hang time for his 414-foot blast was a preposterous 6.1 seconds, long enough for Trea Turner to round the bases twice.

As if to underline the D.C. mythology of Zimmerman's blow, Dodgers power hitter Max Muncy crushed what looked like a long home run to center in the eighth inning, a shot that sent Michael A. Taylor to the wall, looking up, before he had to dash in a few feet to make the catch.

"I was just hoping it didn't hit that wall of wind," General Manager Mike Rizzo said. "But when Zim hits 'em, they stay hit."

"He's a beast," fellow Nats first baseman Matt Adams explained.

As usual, Zimmerman tried to be modest — always the same approach, don't try to do too much: "Got on top of a high fastball — finally." But then he said: "This is what we live for. . . . No, I can't explain how those moments feel. You can't replicate it anywhere else. But afterwards, you take some time to cherish it."

Others will, too.

This game, setting up a do-or-die meeting with the possibility of the wild-card winners beating the 106-win, back-to-back pennant-winning Dodgers, had other hair-raising moments. In the seventh inning, an exhausted Scherzer faced left-handed slugger Joc Pederson as Manager Dave Martinez stayed nailed to the top dugout step, even though the Nats' lone lefty, Sean Doolittle, was warm.

Pederson lashed a bases-clearing, three-run double down the right field line — at least that's what they may tell you in L.A. Right field umpire Ted Barrett called it foul. Replay showed that it was foul by perhaps a half an inch. If Barrett had pointed "fair," would there have been enough evidence to reverse the call? We'll never know.

We do know that Scherzer's next pitch, his 109th, produced a groundout, ending the ace's night at seven innings of three-hit, one-run, seven-strikeout

Nationals 6, Dodgers 1

L.A.	AB	R	H	BI	BB	SO	AVG
Pederson rf	4	0	0	0	0	1	.182
Muncy 1b	4	0	0	0	0	0	.286
J.Turner 3b	4	1	1	1	0	0	.333
Bellinger cf	4	0	1	0	0	0	.200
Seager ss	4	0	1	0	0	1	.188
Beaty lf	3	0	1	0	0	0	.400
Freese ph	1	0	1	0	0	0	.571
Lux 2b	3	0	0	0	1	2	.222
Smith c	2	0	0	0	2	1	.111
Hill p	1	0	0	0	0	1	.000
Maeda p	0	0	0	0	0	0	—
Pollock ph	1	0	0	0	0	1	.000
Urias p	0	0	0	0	0	0	.000
Baez p	0	0	0	0	0	0	—
Stripling p	0	0	0	0	0	0	—
C.Taylor ph	1	0	0	0	0	1	.167
May p	0	0	0	0	0	0	—
TOTALS	32	1	5	1	3	8	—

WASHINGTON	AB	R	H	BI	BB	SO	AVG
T.Turner ss	5	2	3	0	0	0	.333
Eaton rf	1	0	0	0	2	0	.200
Rendon 3b	2	1	1	3	0	0	.267
Soto lf	3	0	0	0	1	0	.222
Kendrick 2b	4	1	2	0	0	0	.278
Doolittle p	0	0	0	0	0	0	—
Hudson p	0	0	0	0	0	0	—
Zimmerman 1b	4	1	2	3	0	2	.400
Suzuki c	3	0	0	0	1	1	.000
M.Taylor cf	3	1	2	0	1	0	.429
Scherzer p	3	0	0	0	0	1	.000
Dozier 2b	1	0	0	0	0	1	.000
TOTALS	29	6	10	6	5	5	—

```
L.A. .............. 100  000  000  —  1  5  0
WASH. ........... 001  041  00X  —  6  10  0
```

LOB: Los Angeles 7, Washington 7. **2B:** Seager (1), T.Turner (1). **3B:** T.Turner (1). **HR:** J.Turner (2), off Scherzer; Zimmerman (1), off Baez. **RBI:** J.Turner (5), Rendon 3 (4), Zimmerman 3 (3). **SB:** Bellinger (1).
SF: Rendon 2. **S:** Eaton.
GIDP: Suzuki.
DP: Los Angeles 2 (Seager, Lux, Muncy; J.Turner, Lux, Muncy).

L.A.	IP	H	R	ER	BB	SO	NP	ERA
Hill	2.2	2	1	1	4	2	58	3.38
Maeda	1.1	1	0	0	0	2	20	0.00
Urias	.2	3	3	3	0	0	14	7.36
Baez	.1	2	1	1	1	0	17	13.5
Stripling	1	1	1	1	0	0	17	9.00
May	2	1	0	0	0	1	26	2.70

WASH.	IP	H	R	ER	BB	SO	NP	ERA
Scherzer	7	4	1	1	3	7	109	2.77
Doolittle	1.1	0	0	0	0	0	20	3.86
Hudson	.2	1	0	0	0	1	9	0.00

WP: Scherzer (1-0); **LP:** Urias (0-1).
Inherited runners-scored: Maeda 3-0, Baez 2-2.
IBB: off Scherzer (Smith). **WP:** Stripling.
T: 3:24. **A:** 36,847 (41,313).

Nationals starting pitcher Max Scherzer pitches in the rain in the seventh inning. (John McDonnell/The Washington Post)

ball. And with that hairbreadth escape, the last big Dodgers push died. "You never know what might've happened," said Dodgers Manager Dave Roberts, "but, shoot, Max threw the heck out of the ball."

Scherzer reduced that split-second and fraction of an inch to the fact that he caught "a break with Pederson."

The implications of this Stay in the Fight victory, which had most of the crowd of 36,847 standing for much more than an hour, from the moment Zimmerman's homer landed, could have lasting ramifications. Why? Because the Dodgers, to the despair of their fan base, are suddenly in deep Dodger Blue doo-doo. The pressure meter in Chavez Ravine has jumped higher than the San Gabriel Mountains.

The Dodgers have a 6-foot-5, 235-pound problem, one with a 0.64 career ERA in the postseason. The new Hollywood horror flick — "Nightmare on Vin Scully Avenue" — is scheduled to open Wednesday, and the lead will be played by Stephen Strasburg, once described by teammate Jayson Werth as "just a big, hairy, scary furry animal."

The Dodgers, for all their money, all their tradition and, at times, all their haughty vanity, have found more ways than their oldest fan has fingers and toes to avoid winning a World Series since 1988.

Now, from the 101 to the Slauson Cutoff, from the hours-long traffic jams on Interstate 5 to the smoggy vastness of the city's banal suburban sprawl, one name will be on every baseball tongue: Strasburg, who fanned 10 Dodgers in six innings of Game 2 on just two days' rest after winning the wild-card game with three innings of relief.

What's Mr. Hairy Scary going to do on full rest?

"We got another game to play," said Strasburg, adding that after his relief stint six days ago, he's finally back on his regular routine and feels "real good" for a start on full rest.

For 137 days, the Nationals have shared huge grins and secret handshakes, group hugs and shimmy shakes, victories and glee. What once looked like a lost season suddenly turned into a month-after-month dugout dance party. After 93 regular season wins, a wild-card game comeback victory and now a pair of comebacks to even this NLDS, the music still hasn't stopped for these Nats. The fight they've stayed in for so long will now go the distance with the Dodgers.

As the Nats took the field for the ninth, the stadium PA system blasted the Beastie Boys: "You've got to fight / For your right / To party!" The fight goes on for a few more days. The party could follow.

GOMES
10
Nationals
22
Emirates FLY BETTER
Emirates FLY BETTER

With grand slam, Nats finally break through

Howie Kendrick gets a hug from Gerardo Parra after his grand slam in the 10th inning. (John McDonnell/The Washington Post)

By Jesse Dougherty

It was a fastball that ran right into his bat, the kind of pitch you dream about in the backyard growing up, with the bases juiced and everything riding on what happens next. So Howie Kendrick used it to make Washington baseball history. He used it to hit a grand slam, shattering a tie in the 10th inning at Dodger Stadium on Wednesday night, sending the Washington Nationals deeper into October than they've ever been before. That's what he did.

It came at 9:23 p.m. in Los Angeles, on the ninth night of October, marking the exact moment that pushed the Nationals past the first round of the postseason. Finally. They beat the Los Angeles Dodgers, 7-3, in Game 5 of the National League Division Series, and this is what an exorcism looks like on a baseball field: Four players trotting slowly around the bases while Joe Kelly shook his head on the mound. Their teammates spilling out of the dugout, stumbling onto the dirt, smiling and screaming and soon smacking Kendrick on the back once he crossed the plate. Then Kendrick hugging Manager Dave Martinez, his helmet torn off his bald head, his fists clenched and his shoulders shaking because this run wasn't going to end like all the others.

And there was later that final sound, an eerie quiet inside the ballpark, ushering the Nationals into a cramped clubhouse that they'd soak with Campo Viejo champagne and cheap light beer. The offense did little against Dodgers starter Walker Buehler for 6⅔ innings. Then came back-to-back homers for Anthony Rendon and Juan Soto off Clayton Kershaw in the eighth, tying the game in two pitches, setting up Kendrick to change, well, everything with a single swing.

"I can't ever describe that," Kendrick said in the middle of the Nationals' third clubhouse celebration in three weeks. "It's just one of the greatest moments of my career. Being able to come through in that situation, it's what we dream of."

Before Kendrick discussed this, before he tried to say how it felt, General Manager Mike Rizzo yelled his name — drawing out a long "Hoooooowie! Are you kidding me?!"— while dumping champagne on his head. Max Scherzer, the team's ace, the pitcher who threw seven innings in Game 4 to make this possible, walked out of the clubhouse with his face in his hands. His eyes were red and dripping with alcohol. He came back moments later wearing ski goggles.

Closer Sean Doolittle held a Star Wars light saber. Shortstop Trea Turner wore an North Carolina State football helmet while he floated through the fray. Yan Gomes wound up shirtless with a cheeseburger in his hand. Fernando Rodney ate an ear of corn. Daniel Hudson stood by the door, a Bud Light in his hand, sipping it slowly because he's flying to Phoenix on Thursday where his wife is expected to give birth to their third child.

This is what relief looked like. This was years of playoff heartbreak crumbled into an unchained celebration, another unchained celebration, each one stretching the concept of what's possible for this team. The past wasn't on the Nationals' side until the end, even after momentum flipped, even after Rendon and Soto made it okay to believe that this year could offer a new script. It never is once the calendar turns to autumn. Not until now.

The Nationals had been to the playoffs in four of the last eight years — 2012, 2014, 2016 and 2017 — but never punched past the division series. Three of those defeats came in a do-or-die Game 5. Each one strengthened the narrative that this club shrinks whenever the stakes grow. But this year was different. The Nationals weren't favored against the 106-win Dodgers. They had house money and Stephen Strasburg on the mound. They've had to win for months now, or so they believed, ever since they sunk to 19-31 and chose to fight instead of fold.

"For the fans who showed up through all those miserable days that we had

Nationals 7, Dodgers 3 (10)

WASHINGTON	AB	R	H	BI	BB	SO	AVG
T.Turner ss	4	0	0	0	1	2	.280
Eaton rf	4	1	0	0	1	1	.158
Rendon 3b	5	3	3	1	0	0	.350
Soto lf	4	2	2	2	1	0	.273
Kendrick 2b	5	1	1	4	0	2	.261
Doolittle p	0	0	0	0	0	0	---
Zimmerman 1b	5	0	1	0	0	3	.333
Suzuki c	1	0	0	0	1	0	.000
Gomes pr-c	2	0	1	0	0	1	.167
M.Taylor cf	5	0	1	0	0	2	.333
Strasburg p	1	0	0	0	1	1	.000
Cabrera ph	1	0	0	0	0	0	.111
Rainey p	0	0	0	0	0	0	---
Corbin p	0	0	0	0	0	0	.000
Adams ph	1	0	0	0	0	1	.000
Hudson p	0	0	0	0	0	0	---
Dozier ph-2b	1	0	0	0	0	0	.000
TOTALS	**39**	**7**	**9**	**7**	**5**	**13**	**—**

L.A.	AB	R	H	BI	BB	SO	AVG
Pederson rf	4	1	2	0	0	1	.267
Pollock ph	1	0	0	0	0	1	.000
Muncy 2b-1b	5	1	1	2	0	0	.263
J.Turner 3b	3	0	0	0	1	0	.286
Bellinger cf	4	0	1	0	0	2	.211
Beaty 1b	3	0	1	0	0	1	.375
Kershaw p	0	0	0	0	0	0	.000
Maeda p	0	0	0	0	0	0	---
Freese ph	1	0	0	0	0	1	.500
Kelly p	0	0	0	0	0	0	---
Jansen p	0	0	0	0	0	0	---
Seager ss	4	0	0	0	0	3	.150
Hernandez lf-2b	4	1	2	1	0	1	.429
Smith c	4	0	0	0	0	1	.077
Buehler p	2	0	0	0	0	1	.000
C.Taylor lf	2	0	0	0	0	0	.125
TOTALS	**37**	**3**	**7**	**3**	**1**	**12**	**—**

```
WASHINGTON.......000  001  020   4  —  7  9  1
L.A...................210  000  000   0  —  3  7  1
```

E: Kendrick (3), Seager (1). LOB: Washington 8, Los Angeles 6. 2B: Rendon 2 (3), Pederson (2). HR: Rendon (1), off Kershaw; Soto (2), off Kershaw; Kendrick (1), off Kelly; Muncy (3), off Strasburg; Hernandez (1), off Strasburg. RBI: Soto 2 (6), Rendon (5), Kendrick 4 (5), Muncy 2 (7), Hernandez (3). SB: Bellinger 2 (3). DP: Washington 1 (T.Turner, Zimmerman); Los Angeles 1 (Muncy, Seager, Beaty).

WASHINGTON	IP	H	R	ER	BB	SO	NP	ERA
Strasburg	6	6	3	3	1	7	105	2.40
Rainey	2	0	0	0	0	0	7	9.00
Corbin	1.1	0	0	0	0	3	22	7.88
Hudson	1	1	1	0	0	0	11	0.00
Doolittle	1	0	0	0	0	1	12	2.70

L.A.	IP	H	R	ER	BB	SO	NP	ERA
Buehler	6.2	4	1	1	3	7	117	0.71
Kershaw	1	2	2	2	0	1	6	7.11
Maeda	1	0	0	0	0	3	14	0.00
Kelly	1.1	3	4	4	2	2	32	23.1
Jansen	2	0	0	0	0	0	6	0.00

WP: Hudson (1-0); LP: Kelly (0-1).
Inherited runners-scored: Kershaw 2-0, Jansen 1-0.
IBB: off Kelly (Soto). HBP: Buehler (Suzuki), Corbin (J.Turner).
T: 4:06. A: 54,159 (56,000).

From left, Stephen Strasburg, Ryan Zimmerman and Brian Dozier in the sudsy postgame locker room. (John McDonnell/The Washington Post)

early: Hey, thank you, appreciate it," Martinez said after the win. "And, yeah, we're playing for a National League championship. A lot of fun."

The minor details will always be overshadowed by the finish: Strasburg gave up three early runs, on two homers, but settled in to finish six innings on 105 pitches. He gave the Nationals a chance at another comeback. It began with Soto and Rendon, like it so often has, once Rendon doubled in the sixth and Soto singled him in. Then the Nationals chased Buehler from the game. Then came Kershaw, one of the best pitchers of this generation, only to give up two homers and the lead.

Rendon lined his to left field. Soto hit a moonshot to right. He spread his arms out as he rounded first, looking like a human airplane, lurching his teammates into a frenzy in the dugout. Patrick Corbin entered out of the bullpen, just two days after a disastrous relief appearance, and recorded four outs. Hudson got the next three to force extra innings. And that's when the Nationals really clicked.

"To win these types of games against this type of team, the Los Angeles Dodgers, your stars have to be stars," Rizzo said. "Our stars were stars tonight, and I think that carried

us through."

Adam Eaton worked a full-count walk against the erratic Kelly. Rendon smacked a double when Manager Dave Roberts chose to keep Kelly in. The Dodgers intentionally walked Soto, bringing Kendrick up, and that's when the 36-year-old took it 410 feet over the center field fence. He had had a rough series to that point, with three errors in five games. He grounded into a double play to kill a rally in the sixth Wednesday night. But baseball has a way of offering another chance.

These Nationals may know that better than anyone. They learned it when they turned their season around in late May. They learned it when they were four outs away from losing the wild-card game last week. And they learned it again right here, in the exact kind of night that has always slipped away from them, now tilted in their favor because Kendrick had the final swing.

"As a hitter, you're like, 'Man, they're really going to do that?'" Kendrick said of the Dodgers walking Soto to get to him. "You want to go out and try to make them pay."

Now the Nationals head to play the Cardinals and see what magic is left. Now they'll test their fate all over again.

Juan for the money

Juan Soto drove in the tying runs with a single in the eighth inning,
and an error allowed the winner. (John McDonnell/The Washington Post)

By Thomas Boswell

All season the Washington Nationals have fought from behind. All season the Nats have overcome decisions that were dubious, or downright disastrous, on who should be called on to pitch. All season, they have looked for their next unlikely hero or an old hero — any ol' hero will do — to turn what looked like a ruined season in May into the beginning of a magical October ride.

On Tuesday night in Nationals Park, the entire Nats season, all 162 games of it, was recapitulated in just nine thrilling, emotionally exhausting innings as Washington rallied from a two-run deficit with three runs in the eighth inning to beat Milwaukee, 4-3, in a National League wild-card game that will assuage the hurt hereabout from three previous Game 5s in division series in this park.

To give extra power and symbolism to their inspiring win, the Nats beat the man who epitomizes the Brewers — Josh Hader, the left-handed reliever who struck out a preposterous 138 men in $75^2/_3$ innings.

Bring on the Dodgers in the NL Division Series that starts Thursday in Los Angeles. They're the team that has ruled the NL with back-to-back pennants but also the club that the Nats, behind their hands, have said they believe they can match, toe-to-toe, in a five-game series. For their past 112 games — as they went 74-38 — the Nats tried to set the stage for that showdown. Now they've got it.

The Nats won with grit, with a hit batsman, with a bloop hit, with a walk and with a rocket of a two-run base hit by Juan Soto, who had been in a 5-for-47 slump that would numb the competitive soul of most 20-year-olds.

Finally, on that Soto hit, the Nats won with a bad hop — which deflected off the glove of Milwaukee right fielder Trent Grisham for an error that brought home the winning run. In other words, they won as they have all season — just as rationality and normal baseball expectations said they would not.

An early-arriving, always-roaring, usually standing and never-give-up crowd of 42,993 did its best imitation of a joyful madhouse as Soto's hit and Grisham's boot cleared the loaded bases and turned 3-1 misery into 4-3 jubilation within seconds. The Nats have practice saving their season, time after time, since they bottomed at 19-31 on May 23. Why would they forget how now?

All season, the Nats have been defined by their resilience — but also by their cussedness. All of those blown leads by their worst-in-baseball bullpen have made them stubborn in the late innings, determined to compensate for their flaw. This time, it was Hader, who strikes out as high a percentage of the hitters he faces as almost any pitcher in history, that the Nats had to defy.

Hader started that indelible eighth by fanning Victor Robles. But he didn't strike out pinch hitter Michael A. Taylor. He hit him with a pitch — a call that was upheld after a Milwaukee challenge that the ball had struck the knob of Taylor's bat first before it hit his hand. By the 10th replay, it looks as if the ball hits bat and hand simultaneously — a perfect tie. So, the original call stands. That's the margin of error — basically nothing — by which a rally that saves a season starts.

After Trea Turner struck out, it seemed the baseball world had been restored to order. One more Nats whiff, and the inning would be over with only the ninth inning left to traverse — a normal two-inning save task for Hader.

But the southpaw did not strike out pinch hitter Ryan Zimmerman, clutch hitter supreme in his youth and prime but now a tough old vet begging his body to let him play a few more games. With two outs, Zimmerman shattered his bat but dumped a beautiful, humpbacked flare into center field for a single. At first base, a sheepish Zim smiled.

Keep the line moving, and the heart beating, any way you can.

And Hader, with his laser fastball and sweeping breaking ball, did not strike out Anthony Rendon, either. As the crowd chanted, "MVP! MVP!" throughout his at-bat, he worked a walk to load the bases. Are you feeling it yet? Are you remembering where you were, whether you watched it at Nationals Park or on TV live or, for the poor unfortunates, when you only saw it on replay?

Above all, Hader did not strike out Soto, the kind of left-handed hitter he is supposed to dominate, intimidate and fit for a dunce cap.

Instead, Soto lashed a rocket to right field on a letter-high fastball, a 100-plus-mph bullet that was certain to be a two-run, game-tying blow. Taylor and swift young pinch runner Andrew Stevenson were sure to score.

That's when the bad hop happened — the best bad hop in Washington baseball since the one in the final inning of the 1924 World Series when Earl McNeely's bouncer hit a rock — a stone or pebble that some searched for for days — and jumped over the head of Giants third baseman Freddie Lindstrom as the winning Senators run dashed home in the 12th inning. You don't have to remind me. A photo of that moment dominates my Facebook page.

Grisham, 22, a rookie with 51 games in the majors who was playing because injured superstar Christian Yelich is out for the season, decided, in the fraction of a second that baseball allows, to charge Soto's hit, hoping to grab it on the first bounce and fling it home. It was probably a futile idea. If Grisham had a voice of experience in his head, it would have screamed, "BE CAREFUL." But hope, blind dumb hope, in the instant when your team's 3-1 lead is turning into a 3-3 mess, seldom holds away.

Grisham raced in at the edge of recklessness. And Soto's drive, with side spin or perhaps an imperfection in the outfield, skidded to Grisham's right, off the edge of his glove and — trickle, trickle, like blood dripping — traveled toward the right field warning track.

By the time Grisham could fetch the nefarious sphere and fling it back to the infield, Rendon had sped home all the way from first base with the fourth — and winning — run.

The Washington bullpen, which, as the world knows, has never done anything right in its collective existence, turned to Daniel Hudson, the trade-deadline addition of General Manager Mike Rizzo. All he did was nail down the save, allowing only a single and getting the last out on a solid fly to jubilant, retreating center fielder Robles.

This three-run rally, which will loom larger the longer the Nats stay alive in these playoffs, was also a reprieve for the Nats decision-makers for what would have been a long cold winter of second-guessing — by others, but, probably, in their darker and most honest moments, of themselves.

For 10 days, at least, Washington fans have debated: Max or Stras? Who should start this wild-card game, Max Scherzer, the three-time Cy Young Award legend but injured much of the second half of the season and dragging a 6.11 ERA in his past three starts? Or Stephen Strasburg, 18-6 this year and roaring to the wire with a 1.76 ERA in his past nine starts?

The Nats picked wrong. But they survived it.

Scherzer walked the first batter of the game, then grooved a first-pitch fastball to the second Brewer — Yasmani Grandal, who bashed it into the Nats' bullpen in right field for a 2-0 lead.

Then, to start the second inning, a soft Scherzer curveball looked tasty to Eric Thames, who smashed it over the right field scoreboard for another home run and a 3-0 lead. A Turner solo homer in the third off Brewers starter Brandon Woodruff was the Nats' only early rebuttal.

As if to turn this game into a kind of baseball laboratory experiment — one that would not satisfy the scientific method but will certainly animate a thousand water cooler debates for months — Strasburg relieved Scherzer after five shaky innings. Where Max was in constant trouble, stranding men in scoring position in three innings, Strasburg breezed through three dominant innings, allowing two hits and no walks and fanning four while making Brewers hitters look silly at times.

Now, it doesn't matter. Now the Nats move on to Los Angeles with $140 million free agent lefty Patrick Corbin on normal rest to face the Dodgers. Like several wild-card winners before them, the Nats arrive with the mystique of a pressure win in a the-season-is-almost-lost comeback.

No, this franchise and this fan base have never had such a win before — to set off an infield celebration and a clubhouse champagne bath for all. Are such wins contagious?

Victories such as this, rallies such as this against, perhaps, the toughest reliever the Nats will face in the whole postseason build a sense of mojo rising, of dreams coming into focus, for a hot team.

For weeks, the Nationals have said that they are clicking so well and enjoying one another's grinning rowdy company so much that they just want to keep on playing. What a magnificent way they chose to prove just how much. And for who knows how long?

Clutch hit, odd bounce, amazing comeback

Juan Soto (22) and his teammates erupt
in joy after rallying past the Brewers.
(John McDonnell/The Washington Post)

By Jesse Dougherty

Juan Soto stood in the middle of the infield, his helmet ripped off his head, his arms punching the air as the Nationals Park crowd of nearly 43,000 leaped and high-fived and screamed all around him.

He had just smacked a two-out single to right field in the eighth inning, and the ball skipped through the grass before trickling off Trent Grisham's glove. Three runners came around to score. The Washington Nationals took a 4-3 lead, and that held as the winning margin in the National League wild-card game Tuesday night. The victory pushed the Nationals into the NL Division Series, a best-of-five fight with the Dodgers that will begin Thursday night in Los Angeles.

And it made Soto, 20, teeming with star power, the hero in a moment that almost never happened.

The Nationals were nearly buried when Max Scherzer gave up three runs on two homers in the first two innings. They couldn't touch the Brewers' bullpen almost all night, flailing against Brent Suter and Drew Pomeranz for three innings, failing to scratch the scoreboard outside Trea Turner's third-inning homer off starter Brandon Woodruff.

But they stayed in it. They rallied against Josh Hader, the Brewers' flame-throwing left-handed reliever, with one out in the eighth. It began with Michael A. Taylor getting hit by a pitch. It continued with two outs, with Ryan Zimmerman at the plate, when the 35-year-old flared a broken-bat single into shallow center. Then Hader walked Anthony Rendon on a 3-2 pitch to bring Soto to the plate. The lefty-lefty matchup favored the pitcher.

The result sent the ballpark into delirium. It left the Nationals' bench spilled onto the field, grabbing at one another's jerseys, watching Soto step onto the grass and roar back at the crowd that was showering him with every bit of noise it could muster.

"You know when you get goose bumps?" Soto said of how he felt once his single landed in the outfield. "That's how I feel. Since I hit the base hit, I got some goose bumps."

The lasting images of the Nationals' night will be their second champagne-soaked celebration in a week. It will be Soto, drenched in Budweiser and bubbles, trying to yell over the music as reporters peppered him with questions. It will be the young outfielder, still too young to legally drink alcohol, reaching into the recycling bin for an empty bottle to hold while he danced with his teammates. It will be him gripping his father's shoulder, his face a spitting image of his old man's, while he did a TV interview immediately after the game. It will be reliever Sean Doolittle, goggles strapped to his face, holding a Star Wars light saber while he hugged Scherzer and told him, "We [expletive] did it again."

But the lasting images were nearly far less happy. They were nearly not happy at all. They were nearly just like the rest of the autumns here, finishing in harrowing defeat, because the Nationals had dropped the other three elimination games they had played here since 2012. The end of the season — one that started so poorly, then arrived in October with a full head of steam — was almost Scherzer, their ace, their unquestioned leader, whipping around to watch a baseball sail over the wall. Twice. There had been doubt about whether Scherzer should start in the first place. He missed six weeks this summer with a string of injuries, including a mid-back strain, bursitis in the scapula below his right shoulder and, finally, a mild rhomboid muscle strain that stole a month.

But the Nationals went with Scherzer, their best pitcher for the past half-

Nationals 4, Brewers 3

MILWAUKEE	AB	R	H	BI	BB	SO	AVG
Grisham rf	3	1	0	0	1	2	.231
Grandal c	3	1	1	2	1	1	.246
Moustakas 3b	4	0	0	0	0	1	.254
Hiura 2b	4	0	1	0	0	3	.303
Spangenberg 2b	0	0	0	0	0	0	.232
Braun lf	4	0	1	0	0	0	.285
Hader p	0	0	0	0	0	0	.000
Thames 1b	4	1	2	1	0	1	.247
Cain cf	4	0	1	0	0	1	.260
Arcia ss	4	0	1	0	0	1	.223
Woodruff p	0	0	0	0	0	0	.267
Shaw ph	0	0	0	0	1	0	.157
Suter p	0	0	0	0	0	0	.000
Pomeranz p	1	0	0	0	0	1	.000
Gamel lf	1	0	0	0	0	0	.248
TOTALS	32	3	7	3	3	11	—

WASHINGTON	AB	R	H	BI	BB	SO	AVG
Turner ss	4	1	1	1	0	1	.298
Eaton rf	3	0	0	0	0	1	.279
Zimmerman ph	1	0	1	0	0	0	.257
Stevenson pr	0	1	0	0	0	0	.367
Hudson p	0	0	0	0	0	0	---
Rendon 3b	3	1	0	0	1	1	.319
Soto lf	4	0	1	2	0	2	.282
Kendrick 1b	3	0	1	0	0	0	.344
Cabrera 2b	3	0	0	0	0	0	.323
Suzuki c	3	0	0	0	0	0	.264
Robles cf	3	0	1	0	0	2	.255
Scherzer p	1	0	0	0	0	0	.182
Dozier ph	1	0	0	0	0	0	.238
Strasburg p	0	0	0	0	0	0	.167
M.Taylor ph-rf	0	1	0	0	0	0	.250
TOTALS	29	4	5	3	1	7	—

```
MILWAUKEE............... 210   000   000   —   3 7 2
WASHINGTON............. 001   000   03X   —   4 5 0
```

E: Moustakas (12), Grisham (0). **LOB:** Milwaukee 6, Washington 3. **2B:** Thames (23), Hiura (23). **HR:** Grandal (28), off Scherzer; Thames (25), off Scherzer; Turner (19), off Woodruff. **RBI:** Grandal 2 (77), Thames (61), Turner (57), Soto 2 (110). **S:** Woodruff. **DP:** Washington 1 (Rendon, Turner, Kendrick).

MILWAUKEE	IP	H	R	ER	BB	SO	NP	ERA
Woodruff	4	2	1	1	0	3	52	3.62
Suter	1	1	0	0	0	1	27	0.49
Pomeranz	2	0	0	0	0	2	30	2.39
Hader	1	2	3	2	1	2	30	2.62

WASHINGTON	IP	H	R	ER	BB	SO	NP	ERA
Scherzer	5	4	3	3	3	6	77	2.92
Strasburg	3	2	0	0	0	4	34	3.32
Hudson	1	1	0	0	0	1	11	1.44

WP: Strasburg, (18-6); **LP:** Hader, (3-5); **S:** Hudson, (6). **HBP:** Hader (M.Taylor). **T:** 2:55. **A:** 42,993 (41,313).

Ryan Zimmerman kept the Nationals alive in the eighth inning with a broken-bat single (John McDonnell/The Washington Post)

decade, the pitcher who has so often lifted this club onto his shoulders. He didn't do that Tuesday. He wilted by giving up a two-run homer to Yasmani Grandal in the first and a solo shot to Eric Thames in the second.

Stephen Strasburg, whom many wanted to start instead of Scherzer, stretched a bit in the bullpen. But he didn't throw any pitches before Scherzer's spot in the batting order came up in the third. That was Manager Dave Martinez's first chance to hook Scherzer and use a batter off his eight-man bench. But the ace finished five innings before Strasburg jogged in from the bullpen, and the questions were already piling up as the right-hander lumbered toward the mound: Was it too late? Was there time for him to clean up Scherzer's mess and keep a slim deficit from growing? Or was Martinez's initial decision just the beginning of the end?

"To go down 3-0 against that bullpen, the way that they were set up in this game, them getting out to an early lead, it's not ideal," Zimmerman said. "But we just tried to fight back. It was . . . just keep going, keep going."

The answers arrived in a slow stream: Strasburg blanked the Brewers for three innings, keeping the Nationals two runs behind. And, finally, up came Soto

with the bases loaded and two outs in the eighth. Soto dug into the batter's box with the crowd on its feet. The scouting report for Hader was to "sell out" on his fastball, just not if it was too high, only if it was around the hands or lower. Hitting coach Kevin Long told Soto to zero in on that pitch and see if he could get it early in the count.

Soto did get it. He lifted a line drive to right, scoring Taylor, pinch runner Andrew Stevenson and Rendon. Soon Daniel Hudson recorded the final three outs, just minutes after the go-ahead hit, and red fireworks shot into the air above the ballpark.

"Once he hit it, I thought, 'Oh, I'm definitely scoring,'" said Stevenson, who was leading off second, his red eyes growing wider with each word. "Then I saw it hit off Grisham's glove, and I thought, 'Oh, everybody's scoring!'"

The team sprinted out of the dugout and toward Hudson once the final out was safe in Victor Robles's glove in center field. Soto ran in from left, screaming again, but stopped before reaching the infield dirt. He knelt down to the field, the same field that has hosted so much October heartbreak, and slapped his chest twice before joining the celebration. It was, after all, happening because of him.

Need a bigger bandwagon

Victor Robles, a natural leader at 22, helped the Nationals
build a winning chemistry. (John McDonnell/ The Washington Post)

By Thomas Boswell

On Sunday, 36,764 fans came to the final regular season game at Nationals Park to cheer, chant and dress up in jerseys with their favorite players' numbers. Thousands also came in goofy shark hats and bandannas — and even at least one full-body shark costume. Because this game had no meaning in the standings, they came just to give ovations of thanks for months of fun and surprise to every Washington Nationals player who deserved such praise, which in their view was all of them.

The Nats, who will host the National League wild-card game against Milwaukee on Tuesday, won their eighth straight game to give them 93 wins for the season. If you'd foreseen that, or anything close to it, on May 23, you could have turned a small mound of cash into a large hill of bills at the expense of someone in Las Vegas.

According to the Elias Sports Bureau, the Nats' 93 wins are the most for a team that was 12 games under .500 at any point during a season since the 1914 Boston Braves finished 94-59 after being 28-40. That Boston club still has a nickname in baseball lore: the Miracle Braves. They swept the supposedly better Philadelphia Athletics, chocked with Hall of Famers, in the World Series.

Good teams are a dime a dozen. Teams that mortify themselves for 50 games, fall near the bottom of the sport, provoke people (including me) to call for the firing of the manager, then play 74-38 ball — which is about as excellent (.661) as the best major league teams ever play for an extended period — are seriously uplifting.

Before the Nats engage in what is an often cruel one-game season Tuesday, in which either team may advance because of one fabulous play, one comic blunder or one total fluke, we should digest what we've already enjoyed for the past 112 games. Because, unless you plan to live another 105 years, you're probably never going to see anything quite comparable again.

Luckily for us, such tales are usually about something extra — a special component — in addition to normal baseball stuff. That's one of the game's gifts. This Nats season was about the power and joy of men from Venezuela to Folsom, La.; from the Dominican Republic to Rapid City, S.D.; from Brazil to Las Vegas, joining in one uninhibited, embrace-our-diversity, summer-long party. It's about Kurt Suzuki, of Japanese and Hawaiian ancestry, dancing Bollywood style in the dugout after hitting a home run "in honor of some of my Indian friends." It's about getting Stephen Strasburg to smile, dance and accept a group hug.

On Sunday, I said to Nats closer Sean Doolittle, "They ought to change the name of this team to the Washington Internationals."

Doolittle started laughing and said: "That's right. It's absolutely a strength of ours — 100 percent. We didn't start winning until Gerardo Parra came in May. We're lucky to have these guys here — the Latin guys.

"There's something about the way this group clicks. The clubhouse is one big comfort zone. [The Latin players] bring energy. They have fun. They put other people at ease. People come out of their shell. We did not have that last year — for sure. The chemistry wasn't there."

Of course, having a veteran who chooses "Baby Shark" as his walk-up song has a way of making everyone act silly. It probably doesn't hurt that he drives a yellow scooter to the ballpark — and sometimes around the clubhouse.

Every team in the majors looks for every edge from analytics, but how do you turn human interaction — clubhouse chemistry — into wins?

In the past two years, the Nats and General Manager Mike Rizzo have tried to crack the code. They hired a manager they thought matched the task, then last winter they grabbed every "high character" or "team leader" or "glue guy" on the market. Pitcher Aníbal Sánchez, catchers Suzuki and Yan Gomes and infielder Brian Dozier fit the bill. Revered Howie Kendrick returned from injury. Rookie Victor Robles, a natural leader at 22, went straight into the starting lineup. Also, a few players who departed may have been addition by subtraction.

In April and May, the Nats gazed, perplexed, at their chemistry beaker — which already had well-respected leaders such as Max Scherzer, Adam Eaton, Doolittle and, in their own ways, Anthony Rendon, Trea Turner and Juan Soto, just 20. Not a bad apple in the barrel. Yet the combination was inert.

Then the Nats picked up castoff Parra because injuries had left them desperate for a warm, professional outfield body. The Nats weren't trying to be brilliant, though Rizzo knew Parra from his Arizona days. In his second game, Parra had a pinch-hit grand slam. This was no shock from a man with 1,312 career hits, two Gold Gloves and $42 million in salaries.

What stunned the Nats was Parra himself. Just by being himself, he demanded, playfully, that everyone have fun, almost all the time. He hugged after hits. He and Sánchez cooked up the dugout dance party after every home run. Parra wore funky, pink-tinted sunglasses throughout the game. Soon, Sánchez was next to him in orange-tinted specs — standing on the top step for three hours, studying the game, chattering, joking, getting teammates involved in talking baseball during the game — even on days they didn't play.

Soon, every Nat who got a single turned to the dugout and made a tiny gesture with his thumb and index finger — like a Baby Shark biting. For a double, they made their whole hand a Mama Shark snapping jaw. For a homer, the Nats made huge chomping Daddy Shark motions with both arms.

The whole crowd joined in. Soon cheesy, cheerful shark gear appeared.

Somehow, the mystery of human interaction, the personalities of Sánchez and Parra, both from Venezuela, empowered all the other Latin players — Soto, Robles and Wander Suero from the Dominican Republic and Gomes from Brazil — to let out all the energy and joy that is ingrained in the béisbol cultures of their countries. Later, Fernando Rodney of the Dominican Republic and another Venezuelan, Asdrúbal Cabrera, joined the mix.

I first encountered this phenomenon 40 years ago doing a series of stories on winter ball in Puerto Rico, then a couple of years later I went to Cuba, too, and eventually the Dominican Republic. I always came back saying: "That kind of joy, that love of detail and subtlety in play, that sense of style is how baseball should be played. That is how fans should be totally engaged, cheering on every pitch — because the count changed. They 'get' the game we invented better than we do. Cool."

To every wonderful or awful twist of the season, humiliation or glory, Parra would shrug and say, "That's baseball." A worldview in two words. The sport — not known for its playfulness toward those who try to master it — wrapped Parra in a hideous 3-for-51 slump in mid-August that left him without an RBI for 45 days. On Thursday, after the Nats had clinched a playoff spot, Martinez put Parra, usually a sub or pinch hitter, in the lineup every day to get him "fixed" so he, his glove, bat and energy could justifiably be part of the playoff roster.

In his last at-bat Thursday, he got a single. In 45 hours, from Friday night through Sunday afternoon, Parra — the man who went 45 days without an RBI — went 7 for 9 and drove in 11 runs.

"That's baseball," Doolittle quipped.

The Nats haven't invented anything new. Other fine teams have had an almost magical camaraderie, such as the 2017 world champion Houston Astros and the Boston Red Sox winners with David Ortiz at their center. Long ago, Joe Morgan, Tony Perez and Pete Rose assigned themselves the job of unifying the Big Red Machine. Many great teams have been jubilant, resilient melting pots.

Of course, in these October matters, hitting, fielding and pitching — such as three-time Cy Young Award winner Scherzer starting Tuesday night — count for a little bit, too. You can't just cheer and dance your way to a ring.

Some teams want to advance in the postseason for achievement and glory. No doubt, the Internationals do, too. But some teams are having such a fine time playing together that they just don't want to come in for supper because it's getting dark earlier. Hey, Mom, we want to keep playing! And the only way big leaguers are allowed to do that is to keep winning.

"Such a fun group," Doolittle said. "We're not ready for it to end."

F-16s from the 113th Wing of the D.C. Air National Guard fly over Nationals Park during Opening Day ceremonies March 28. (Ricky Carioti/The Washington Post)

How can the Nationals lose Harper and get better? It's fundamental, really.

By Thomas Boswell

Southpaw Patrick Corbin, who fanned 246 batters last season, and catcher Yan Gomes, who hit 16 homers, were all-stars at last season's game at Nationals Park.

Brian Dozier, Trevor Rosenthal and Kurt Suzuki also have been all-stars. Dozier hit 42 and 34 homers in 2016 and 2017, respectively. Rosenthal, just 28, saved 45 and 48 games in consecutive seasons and was a standout in a World Series. In the past two years in 623 at-bats, Suzuki hit 31 homers with 100 RBI and an .825 on-base-plus-slugging percentage.

Aníbal Sánchez and Max Scherzer were teammates in Detroit from 2012 to 2014. And when Scherzer won his first Cy Young in 2013, Sánchez won the ERA title (2.57) that season. Last year, Sánchez's ERA was 2.83.

In the past two years, in 645 at-bats, Matt Adams has 41 homers and 122 RBI. In his career, Kyle Barraclough has a 3.21 ERA with 279 strikeouts in 218²/₃ innings.

All of them are new Washington Nationals, all added in one offseason.

Sometimes I'm not entirely sure everyone is paying full attention. Especially when I see Las Vegas odds say the Nats are in a three-way tie as the ninth-best team in MLB with mundane 16-1 odds to win the World Series.

"You look at this team, and there really isn't a weakness," said Corbin, who signed a six-year, $140 million contract as a free agent, which remains more money than the next two most lucrative signings of this offseason combined.

The Nats will have everything they can handle — and maybe more — just to win the National League East from the defending champ Braves and the much-improved Phillies and Mets. It should be a lovely six-month battle.

With so many games against tough division rivals, it will be especially tough for NL East teams to win enough games to get a wild-card spot. So this could get ugly. That's why it's easy to lump the Nats, minus the flashy Bryce Harper, who hasn't been in the Nats' plans for months, among the teams with a great deal to prove.

But the Nats are also a potentially exceptional team that is now in Florida trying to shed its slipshod ways of 2018 when gruesome defense, air-headed base running, some disappointing starting pitching, unsound fundamentals, a raw rookie manager — is this list long enough? — plus a lot of injuries produced an 82-80 season that Scherzer calls "a terrible year."

"Pitching, defense and athleticism has been our credo for 12 years," said General Manager Mike Rizzo, who thinks his team drifted from those core values. "Last year, there were reasons our defense wasn't very good. Our record in one-run games [18-24] showed it. We gave too many teams 28, 29, 30 outs, and we gave away outs with our base running. This year, we'll be much better. We have to be."

It will help that Daniel Murphy, who started only one double play in 36 starts at second base, has taken his bat to Colorado to play first base. And it will help that Harper, team-spirited enough to play out of position in center field in 63 games, won't be gumming up the works with his starkly deteriorating defense.

Team leadership has been, off and on, an issue for the Nats for years. Every championship club needs at least a half-dozen future managers in its clubhouse to demand accountability and constantly raise the team's baseball IQ. Those players, such as Jayson Werth, may never manage a game anywhere except in Little League for one of their kids. But everyone in the room knows that they could become respected managers if they chose to be.

Last season, after Howie Kendrick was lost for the season to injury, the Nats were down to Scherzer and Adam Eaton as the two fully engaged and demanding team leaders. The night reliever Shawn Kelley showed up Martinez by slamming his glove on the ground and glaring into the dugout after giving up a homer — as if he were a big star who merited better than mop-up duty — people with knowledge of the Nationals say Max and Mighty Mouse were waiting for him in the tunnel after the game to chew him out.

This year, they may have company. Kendrick is back. "He was a huge loss for us," Rizzo said.

Dozier always has been a heady team leader. When the Nats asked Scherzer about Sánchez's clubhouse makeup, Scherzer raved about him being a "great glue guy in the clubhouse" who unites factions and organized team dinners. And he was a savvy teacher, too. "Taught me some things," Scherzer said.

Gomes and Suzuki "check those boxes," according

A Phillies fan at Nationals Park on April 2 wears a mask of Bryce Harper. (Jonathan Newton/The Washington Post)

to Rizzo, as student-of-the-game players who demand alertness and hustle from others.s

Though few mention it, subtracting Harper, while it will cost 34 homers, a .899 career OPS and some amazing hair flips, would help any team improve its attention to fundamentals. When the most famous player on the team can't go 10 days without failing to run out a groundball or overthrowing a cutoff man by 15 feet or throwing to the wrong base or being caught unprepared in the outfield or on the bases, it's hard to demand total alertness from the other 24.

"Write it," one prominent Nats vet said.

Losing Harper carries a high cost. But if the Nats don't play a crisper, less mistake-riddled brand of baseball without him, it's an opportunity wasted. Rizzo has done many things right, but in Bryce's early years, when he had "players' managers" who rarely said a discouraging word and owned no whip, Rizzo should have been the bad cop to tell him the truth about the gaps in his game. But the GM had such a high opinion of Harper personally — always referred to as "such a great kid" — that he couldn't make the leap to "but also an overindulged player."

Perhaps Rizzo and the Nats made a mistake in thinking that a club that tested Dusty Baker's patience could be handled and shaped up by any rookie manager.

Now, a year later, the Nats and Martinez are focused on what should have obsessed them last year in their cheery training camp: basics. You can ride camels and have golf-shot games after you prove you consistently play the game right.

"We're going to be more proactive on fundamentals," Martinez said this week. "There will be days when they don't bring their bats to the field. It will all be team defense, base running and fundamentals. They can still hit in the cage."

Martinez has reiterated his belief that teams don't need to work long hours in spring training if their work is crisp and precise. This year, he's added a twist: "If we don't do it right, then the days will get long." Well, better late than never.

This is a Nats team with few weaknesses, a dominant top three in its rotation and justified reasons for high hopes. But it is also a club that will sink if it repeats its mental gaffes and fundamental laxness from last season's embarrassment.

Out of necessity, improvement. Or that's the idea, anyway.

Sweep by the Mets drops the Nationals to a season-worst 12 games under .500

By Jesse Dougherty

The Washington Nationals overcame a deficit again, recovered when they looked totally lost, pushed ahead with a late rally that seemed, if only for a moment, to take their season off the brink and put it back on life support.

Yet that was just a placeholder for another disaster at Citi Field on Thursday. It was only a matter of time until the bullpen entered, until another effort collapsed in its hands, until the Nationals suffered a 6-4 defeat to the New York Mets and dropped to 19-31 in a season that feels all but entirely lost.

Wander Suero stood by the mound, his shoulders slumped, his eyes trained on the bleachers that swallowed up Carlos Gómez's game-winning three-run homer with two outs in the eighth. It was the newest kind of fall for the Nationals, a team testing just how many ways there are to lose: waste four early rallies with bad situational hitting, wake up when the manager is ejected in the eighth, spring ahead in that same inning, then throw it all away soon after because the bullpen still cannot get outs.

That was it. That was how Washington left New York with four losses, each one more crushing than the last, and the smallest, shrinking window to turn this around. That was supposed to happen here, with the Mets wading through their own issues, looking like a perfect springboard for the Nationals to jump on.

Instead, improbably, the Nationals depart with a five-game losing streak, 10 games out of first place and in a full-on crisis of their own.

"Things are going to change. Things are going to change," repeated Manager Dave Martinez, who watched the end of the loss from the Nationals' clubhouse after being tossed in the eighth. "And I know that. So we just got to keep pounding away, keep playing baseball. There's good players in that clubhouse, really good players. We'll turn things around."

Martinez was up until 2 a.m. Thursday re-watching yet another late-game meltdown in his hotel room. Then he and the Nationals were awake a few hours later, quietly boarding the team bus, driving through morning Manhattan traffic and a light drizzle. The series finale began at 12:10 p.m. The sharp turnaround gave them little time to unwind and unpack Wednesday night's crushing 6-1 defeat. They had another game to play and could take the smallest bit of comfort in that.

But that only brought more problems by day's end. The Nationals started 0 for 9 with runners in scoring position. They wasted a strong seven-inning effort from Stephen Strasburg. They were sparked by Martinez's ejection, then Suero left a 1-2 cutter over the plate, and Gómez circled the bases around him.

"Look, we've got to find a guy in that seventh and eighth to get the ball to [closer Sean] Doolittle," Martinez said of his major league-worst bullpen. "That's the bottom line. In my mind and in my heart, I know we have the guys to do it. We've just got to finish it."

Martinez later insisted that he was just defending Howie Kendrick in the eighth — ejected moments before the manager sprung from the dugout — and wanted home plate umpire Bruce Dreckman to ask for help on a check-swing call. But there were plenty of other sources of frustration, Dreckman aside: an offense that left eight men on base to that point, the fact that they were five outs from being swept and the general disappointment of sinking so far below expectations before the season has reached Memorial Day.

The manager screamed his voice hoarse while pointing in all directions. He kicked dirt onto home plate. He spiked his hat into the batter's box and stomped around. He looked as angry as he has been since leading this team, a job that's now in jeopardy, and maybe it was about time. Washington's bad baseball had seeped into another day and soon another loss and then became another reason to believe that a disappointing start may have just been the introduction to a disappointing team.

Those in the clubhouse won't say that, at least not publicly, at least not while they are still trying to push through. They are baseball players, their lives defined by failure, accustomed to placing irrational confidence in the chance to try again. But those opportunities have dwindled after 50 games. The calendar is no longer their friend. The margin for error, or whatever was left of it, has disappeared.

The Nationals soon left Queens, where they arrived this week in less disarray than the spiraling Mets and left as the bigger mess. The Marlins, winners of six straight, wait for them in Washington. Everything else is way up in the air.

Manager Dave Martinez, ejected in the eighth inning, vowed after the Nationals fell to 19-31, "We'll turn things around." (Julio Cortez/Associated Press)

New York to new life: How a humbling sweep set the Nationals straight

100%
Chance of making
the playoffs
Sept. 24 (88-69)

3%
Chance of making
the playoffs May 23
(19-31 record)

A graphic depicts the Nationals' playoff
chances over the course of the season.

By Jesse Dougherty and Sam Fortier

Dave Martinez's eyes were red, and his face was sticky with grape juice cocktail, but the Washington Nationals manager kept thinking about the date that has been on his mind for months.

"I said it on May 24 ..." Martinez started, and that was enough. He could have stopped right there. He was standing next to two folding tables, looking as if they were fetched from the basement of a fraternity house, covered in champagne and beer cans and a sea of off-white foam. This was the Nationals' clubhouse last Tuesday night. This was the celebration for making the National League wild-card game, and this was their manager remembering how it came so close to not happening.

"I thought we hit the bottom then," Martinez continued, champagne spraying over his head, and he was almost right. The Nationals were 19-31 after they were swept in a four-game series by the New York Mets at Citi Field. They were cooked. Then they climbed back, slowly at first, before becoming the fourth team in history to go from 12 games below .500 to the playoffs.

"And here we are," Martinez finished, and now he was choked up, having drawn a clear line between the season's darkest days and the result of not slipping into them. This is what happened then and how it led to what will happen next, a date with the Milwaukee Brewers at Nationals Park on Tuesday, and a chance to turn their comeback into something more.

Juan Soto and Victor Robles had to be up way earlier than usual. It was May 21, the Tuesday of the Mets series, the morning after a 5-3 loss, and they were expected at the MLB Network studios in Secaucus, N.J.

They rode in an SUV with two team public relations staffers. They marveled at the sets upon arriving. While Robles waited for his turn, off to the side with a producer, he noticed a list of teams on the back wall of the network's Studio 41. He scanned the circles to find the Nationals' logo. Then he noticed something.

"Are those the standings?" Robles asked in Spanish.

"Yeah," the producer answered. "Someone comes in every day to change them, so they are up-to-date."

Robles shook his head. The Nationals were behind the Philadelphia Phillies, the Atlanta Braves and the Mets. They were 19-28. Players aren't supposed to look at the standings during the season, especially not in May. But here was a reminder Robles didn't expect. The young outfielder was a bit quieter until the cameras came to him.

The Nationals lost again that night, 6-5, before Soto and Robles found themselves at the center of the latest meltdown.

Washington led the Mets 1-0 heading into the eighth inning Wednesday. Kyle Barraclough, who was later designated for assignment, recorded two outs but allowed two base runners. That's all teams needed against the Nationals' bullpen early this season. The bullpen's ERA ballooned to a league-worst 6.89 during that week. Martinez soon went to his closer, Sean Doolittle, for four outs. Doolittle hit a batter with a pitch to load the bases. Then he threw a low-and-in fastball that Juan Lagares ripped into the left-center gap.

Soto and Robles chased after it. Both pulled up a few feet from where it landed, neither dived, and the double rattled around the wall while the go-ahead runs scored. Citi Field was delirious. Doolittle, cap tipped up off his head, couldn't wipe a distant stare off his face. He allowed six runs to score without retiring a batter. There were rumblings the next morning, among people in the organization, that either Soto or Robles had to go all out to make the play. It was the only time this season that visible fractures, however small, began to form in the clubhouse.

MLB Network didn't play on the TVs while Washington prepped for the series finale. If it had, or if the Nationals checked social media, the outlook wasn't pretty: Multiple media outlets said Martinez was as good as fired. Articles suggested the club trade Anthony Rendon, a pending free agent, and maybe even Max Scherzer or Doolittle while their value was still high.

"People were just completely jumping ship on us," Doolittle said in September. "I was on the Cubs. I was definitely on the Cubs; I might have been on the Twins for a minute. But I'm glad I came back here. This has been a lot of fun."

The bullpen back then was an entirely failing operation. That was a big part of why pitching coach Derek Lilliquist was fired May 2. Only Doolittle, Wander Suero and Tanner Rainey are still part of the bullpen Washington is taking into the postseason. The Nationals struggled to maintain even the largest leads, and Martinez could only really trust Doolittle. The problem was compounded because every bullpen bet made by General Manager Mike Rizzo in the offseason — Trevor Rosenthal, Tony Sipp, Barraclough — never panned out. A few relievers said they felt the manager leaned heavily on Doolittle and those he thought had potential, such as Barraclough and Suero, because the season, and maybe his job, were in jeopardy.

But they also thought the approach created problems: The "untrustworthy" arms struggled to find a rhythm with few opportunities to earn high-leverage spots. The others were overused because relievers rarely tap out. Bullpens valorize a willingness to take the ball. One veteran recalled that older relievers occasionally went to Martinez's office and told him when younger guys were too tired to pitch. It reached a point that whenever the relievers were together — in the bullpen, in the dugout,

out to eat — and heard anything that sounded like a phone ringing, they jokingly urged Suero to get loose.

One reliever believes this usage was unsustainable and that, if the complete collapse hadn't happened in New York, it would have against another team. Another pitcher thought this team, until then, felt like last year's middling squad. He thought this series changed that and said, "Mediocrity was tolerated; embarrassment wasn't." Yet no one blew up.

"Losers throw tables; losers break things," right fielder Adam Eaton said. "We weren't losers. We never got that desperate."

They did, however, all gather before the series finale Thursday. A few people in the clubhouse recalled that everyone had a chance to say what they thought was wrong. Martinez stays away from mandated meetings. He learned in the twilight of his career, while playing for Bobby Cox on the Atlanta Braves, that the clubhouse belongs to the veterans.

And that's who decided it was time to hash it out before the last game in New York. Martinez sat back and watched. The rest of the staff was in the room, too. A few players thought it was a formality, necessary given the circumstances, a chance for guys to speak and move on. Scherzer, the team's ace and one of its leaders, later described it as "mostly trivial." But others, including some members of the bullpen, felt it was important to put everything on the table. Multiple relievers, according to those in the room, took responsibility for not pulling their weight.

"That can divide teams, when the starters are doing their job and the hitters are scratching runs across and giving you leads late in games and you can't hold them," Doolittle said. "Those are the things that start to erode team chemistry."

Martinez only spoke after everyone had a chance, looking around the quieted room, locking eyes with whoever would stare back.

"Listen to yourselves; you're all saying the same stuff," Martinez recalled telling his players. "You still trust each other."

But even if the air was cleared, even if the Nationals all knew what needed to change, they went out and lost again.

The last and lasting images of the disaster in New York: Martinez kicking dirt onto home plate. Martinez spiking his hat into the batter's box. Martinez stomping around in a tirade that got him ejected in the eighth inning and looked to some like it may have been his last act in a Nationals uniform.

The fire seemed to ignite the Nationals for a moment. They even surged ahead. Then Suero surrendered a three-run homer to Carlos Gómez, and the bullpen had blown it again.

Clubhouses are often quiet after losses. But this was different. The Nationals were in free fall, Martinez was asked who was to blame, and he instead preached this season could be saved. He repeated, in a hoarse voice, his team would go 1-0 tomorrow. The mind-set, at the time, seemed more problematic than prophetic.

"I can remember the moment leaving New York. How could I forget it?" Scherzer said. "It was a really low moment. It was by far the lowest moment of the season."

"It was like: 'That was so bad. Let's get the [expletive] out of here; let's go home,'" Doolittle remembered. "'We need to regroup, but let's get out of here — fast.'"

So they did. The players stuffed their bags quickly. A red clock on the wall ticked. They strode out of the clubhouse, hooked a left, passed through double doors and found their way onto a waiting coach. The bus ferried them west, out of Queens, through Manhattan traffic and finally to Penn Station, where they boarded a chartered Amtrak train. They sank into their seats. Someone passed out pizza as they shoved off.

By the time they arrived in Washington, a few hours later, there was at least one shared feeling in the near-silent cars: Everyone was relieved to be home.

Just the other day, after the beer-soaked celebration, amid an eight-game winning streak to finish the regular season, Martinez reached deep into a desk drawer inside his office at Nationals Park.

He was looking for an old lineup card. A few of his coaches sat in the couches and stadium seats across the room. He wanted everyone to realize how far this team had come. He also wanted a few laughs.

Martinez looked down at the sheet and began reading aloud: "Leading off, Victor Robles . . . batting second, Wilmer Difo . . . batting third, Adam Eaton . . . fourth, Kurt Suzuki . . . fifth, Brian Dozier."

That was the order for a May 5 game in Philadelphia, a few weeks before Washington hit bottom, and a few months later it was buried by their success. But that lineup doubled as evidence of what spurred such a sharp turnaround. The Nationals, first and foremost, were healthy by the start of June. Trea Turner, Rendon and Soto finally played at the same time. Aníbal Sánchez found a rhythm as the fourth starter, complementing a stacked rotation. The bullpen became passable. The Nationals picked on the Miami Marlins the weekend after New York, winning three of four, then went on the best 80-game stretch in club history.

Before that series with the Marlins, when the season was fading, Rizzo stopped in to see Martinez. They didn't talk about his job status. Neither felt the need. Yet Martinez was mindful of expectations that were not being met. He sat at his desk, just a few feet from where he recited that lineup card in late September, and promised Rizzo that the Nationals, despite everything, still had a pulse.

"I told him we would be okay," Martinez recalled. "I gave him my God's honest word, and I believed it."

Stephen Strasburg, shown July 3, pitched seven strong innings May 23, but the bullpen buckled again. (John McDonnell/ The Washington Post)

The Nationals kept believing in Martinez even when no one else did. Including me.

By Thomas Boswell

Two days before the Washington Nationals hit bottom at 19-31, I wrote: "If I were asked whether the Nats should fire Dave Martinez, I would, unhappily and with a sincere desire to be proved wrong, say, 'Probably.'

"If the Nats decide to give Martinez more time, with a healthier lineup and a weak schedule, to get up to $200 million-payroll cruising speed by the All-Star Game, that might work. But ... if lame fundamentals and a poor (and poorly managed) bullpen keep dogging the Nats, then I will understand if the team decides that someone, maybe anyone, would be better ... than Dave Martinez."

There was plenty of praise for Martinez personally but lots of specific criticism of his managing. But you don't care. You want to hear what Martinez's team thinks of him now. Especially, you want context for what comes next as the Nats play the first of 14 remaining games against the defending National League East champion Atlanta Braves on Thursday.

The Nats and Martinez will be tested severely. Maybe the Braves will be, too. But just as the Nats have saved their season, so their manager's prospects have been revived, too. I may get my wish: a "sincere desire to be proved wrong." The Nats players sure think so.

"I like how he didn't change anything. It's funny how things are spun: One day, somebody doesn't know anything; now, he's a genius," said shortstop Trea Turner, whose broken finger and hitting slump when he returned coincided with 50 games when the Nats were 21-29. "He believed in us, and we believed in him."

"It's easy to kick people when they are down: 'It must be the manager's fault,'" catcher Kurt Suzuki said.

"Half our starting lineup was hurt," Suzuki added of the Nats, whose projected Nos. 1-3-4-5 hitters missed 126 games because of injuries. All had rusty slumps after they returned, too. "There was all this outside noise. I'm sure he hears it, but you can never tell. This guy understands the grind. He kept us having fun."

Well, maybe not having fun at 19-31 but not in total chaos, either.

"He didn't panic," closer Sean Doolittle said. "Every day, same kind of even-keel guy. For me, as a vet, I respected that."

What about that historically awful bullpen, which still has the fifth-worst bullpen ERA in the past 65 years?

"Nobody looks like they can run the bullpen well" when the ERA is over 7.00, Suzuki said. "Nobody is talking about how well the bullpen is doing now. Nobody is there to praise them. They're a huge part of why we're winning."

In a stunning reversal, the bullpen ERA has been 2.91 during the current 31-12 streak. In a season in which bullpens everywhere have been torched, only one team has a bullpen ERA better than 3.76 for the whole season.

Perhaps veteran Ryan Zimmerman best sums up both the lousy injured offense and the nervous-breakdown bullpen that turned the eighth inning into the "Evil Dead."

"What was the manager supposed to do exactly?" Zimmerman said. "Managers have an influence. But the game is always about the players. It's always on us."

A big part of the Nats' flip is simply that, as the oldest team in baseball, with 15 players who are 30 and three others 29, they mostly manage themselves.

"We got punched in the mouth early. ... This game will eat you alive. If it's not this veteran group of guys, I don't know if we turn it around," Brian Dozier said recently.

However, no Nat is a bigger booster of Martinez — who, after a 15-year playing career, trusts veterans and helps them endure the downs — than Dozier, who called him this week, "a leader of men because he treats us as adults. ...

"I love managers that played. When the bad times come, they can relate," Dozier added. "When I got my 1,000th hit, Dave walked by and said, 'Only 600 to go.' He meant 600 for me to pass him" with 1,599 hits.

Managers such as Martinez have always been around: well liked, funny at times, doing comical things to loosen up "the boys," being empathetic and making the standard in-game moves. But they seldom have an original approach or motivational knack when things slide, such as starting 19-31 when you have a Big Three at the top of your rotation and Doolittle in the bullpen.

Some of them won pennants, such as Joe Altobelli, Danny Murtaugh, Tommy Lasorda, Charlie Manuel, Dusty Baker, Joe Maddon, Terry Francona and, back in time, Jolly Cholly Grimm and others. Some won World Series. Casey Stengel even won a lot of World Series.

Sean Doolittle said of Manager Dave Martinez, above: "He didn't panic. . . . I respected that." (Jonathan Newton/The Washington Post)

The problem is that plenty of these Just One of the Guys skippers can't manage worth a darn. They just sit in the chair, for years, and are "good guys" or get along with the GM. A team with talent carries them to lots of wins, but they never get over the hump. It can take forever to fire them, such as Danny Ozark or beloved Don Zimmer.

Martinez is a prototype of this genial easy-riding breed. "He's a lot like Gardy: upbeat, jokes a lot," Dozier said, referring to Detroit Tigers Manager Ron Gardenhire, who won division titles with the Minnesota Twins with little visible talent.

"I'd put him up there with every single manager I've had," said Suzuki, 35, who has changed teams five times. "He's everything you want: comfortable, relaxed. When we were pressing a little bit, he kept us loose. 'Be patient.' Take it slowly, didn't look at the standings. Davey's like a player. He jokes around. We bust his [chops] in the dugout during games. He loves it.

"He doesn't have to act like, 'I'm the manager.' He's just himself."

Players trust Martinez's words, even when they have an edge.

"I'm about as honest as I can get," Martinez said this week, almost sheepish to compliment himself for anything. "They might not like everything I have to say. Hopefully, in three, four, five days, they'll respect me for saying it."

We have learned that Martinez is that rare person who can go 212 games into the job he has always wanted, have a fire-the-bum 101-111 record and still not show any angry panic or lost faith either in public or with his team.

The past two months have bought him time to show what he can do. The four games now against the Braves — and the 10 more to follow — will just be the first of many tests. Players who already liked Martinez when they were playing lousy now sound as if they're prepared to believe in him when they're playing their best.

What we don't know yet is whether, over a long season and perhaps multiple years, Martinez is one of the good guys who is also a truly good manager.

Castoff Parra got the Nationals dancing, and the party just kept going strong

By Thomas Boswell

On Tuesday, Gerardo Parra danced with Juan Soto in the Washington Nationals' dugout. On Wednesday, he danced with Matt Adams, hand in hand, doing everything but a twirl. But Thursday, on the Fourth of July, Parra just danced around the bases.

Right now, from his role as team dance maestro and source of joy to his infrequent but valuable time on the field, Parra is the off-the-junk-heap symbol of a Nats team that thinks baseball is the most jubilant, carefree, jump-up-and-dance game in the world, especially when you're on a 26-10 hot streak. Yes, the worry-free, highflying, giddy-happy Nats, who ended Thursday holding the first of two National League wild-card spots at 45-41. Those Nats.

On Independence Day, Parra was freed from the pine for one afternoon to do his Adam Eaton impression — bat second and play right field. He hammed up the part with a double off the top of the left field fence, a double off the scoreboard in right, one run and two RBI in a 5-2 win to complete a three-game sweep of the Miami Marlins.

Parra can also do a good impression of a left-handed-hitting first baseman (Adams), if necessary, as well as a fine facsimile of a strong-armed center fielder (Victor Robles). If asked to be a left-handed pinch hitter, he just imitates himself.

But for all his versatility — and Parra is a gentleman with 1,285 hits, two Gold Gloves and, as recently as last season in Colorado, a $10 million salary — the role he plays best is instigator of innocent joy. Talk about a team that needed it — and got it.

Parra is normally the Nats' 25th man, the least likely fellow to get in a game, but he is the central ingredient in Nationals Dance Party, the celebration line that awaits every home run hitter — but always in the dugout, as Manager Dave Martinez prefers, never on the field where it might show up or motivate foes.

Parra invented the dance line — in which he is always the last person to exchange dance steps with the hero. Heck, Parra is a dance line. The whole deal is intended to be ridiculous, part boast but also self-mocking. It's silly, just like Parra's walk-up song — "Baby Shark," a ditty for toddlers — that has the crowd snapping its arms like sharks as he comes to the plate. Metallica it's not.

With Parra inciting them, the Nats jiggle, wiggle, salsa or, if it's Brian Dozier, do some twerking. Kurt Suzuki did a wonderfully bad hula after pretending to shoot the curl by surfing through a "tube" of his teammates. The Nats don't have a best dancer. That defeats the point. "We're all the best," Robles said.

On Thursday, after a Fernando Rodney save in which the oldest man in baseball — by three years — touched 99 mph, the Nats practically danced off the field, winners of eight out of nine. And, at that moment, a team in a playoff spot.

"I promise you we make the playoffs," Parra said in a grinning TV interview.

Swallow, chew and digest. You can wait many years to enjoy an unexpected six-week baseball feast such as this. The Nats have munched on some weak teams, but, in all, they have thumped a representative bunch.

Standings change every time you blink. But the idea that the dead Nats of late May could be in a playoff spot by the Fourth of July is incredible, bordering on ridiculous. Back then, national pundits counseled the team to consider trading Max Scherzer — and everybody else in sight — by the July 31 deadline because the Nats were so bad they should just blow up their roster and slink away in shame.

Now, in 41 days, the Nats ended their game Thursday having gained a net total of 88 games against the other 14 teams in the National League. In the majors, only the Los Angeles Dodgers have won more games than the Nats during this time. As a tip-off that these healthy Nats probably have legs, only Los Angeles has stomped its foes by more (plus-67 run differential) than the Nats (plus-61).

Of course the Nats have won because Scherzer and Stephen Strasburg rank first and second in the NL in strikeouts, Patrick Corbin is 7-5 with a 3.55 ERA and tricky, speed-changing Aníbal ("Invisi-bal") Sánchez has a 2.14 ERA in his past seven starts. Anthony Rendon has 20 homers in just 72 games, a sign he may have 40-homer years ahead. Juan Soto, 20, has a .946 on-base-plus-slugging percentage, and Sean Doolittle has saved just about everything, including, maybe, Martinez's job.

"Something good happens every day," Gerardo Parra said. "Just enjoy the moment." (Katherine Frey/The Washington Post)

But Parra is the best current symbol of this team because he epitomizes its bench. And that bench has saved this season.

On Opening Day, first baseman Adams, utility hitter Howie Kendrick and catcher Suzuki were not in the lineup. And Parra hadn't been released by the San Francisco Giants, making him, literally, free to the Nats except maybe for meal money.

These four fellows have gotten 601 at-bats this season. Go on, guess how many homers and RBI they have combined. Guess high. No, higher than that. Sorry, you're wrong. Maybe you got "39 homers," but you didn't say "134 RBI." If you wonder why the Nats' offense hasn't missed Bryce Harper too much, it's them.

Parra carries a double symbolism because he is not only an emblem of the bench, but he is also one of the main catalysts of what, at this point, can only be called "team chemistry" aboard a club that had 15 players on Thursday's roster who played little or not at all for the 2018 Nats.

"Sometimes there are just people who help bring a team together. Parra's been in that role — unselfish, lifts the mood," said senior adviser to the general manager Bob Boone, himself an eight-time Gold Glove catcher. "We thought the clubhouse was going to be solid. And it is."

For that, there are many reasons, such as players who have been natural leaders with the Nats or at other stops — Kendrick, Scherzer, Eaton, Dozier, Suzuki, Yan Gomes and, in their ways, the tough Trea Turner and the relaxed Rendon.

But Parra, who hit a grand slam to beat the Dodgers on May 11, his second day in a Nats uniform, then hit a three-run homer to help beat the New York Mets five days later, arrived with a kind of "click." He was a last-ditch prayer of a pickup. He knew it and ate it up. He could sit for a week, then get three hits. But just as importantly he seemed to embody Martinez's preferred mood: Would you guys please relax, have fun and just try to play the game right because you're really good.

"Believe in yourself and be happy," Parra said. "Head up. Something good happens every day. Just enjoy the moment." Excuse me, can I get the book rights?

That attitude may or may not work under October pressure. But it seems to help when you're 19-31, your Nos. 2-3-4-5 hitters are hurt and your bullpen is egregious.

"When we were 19-31, it was eye-opening," Suzuki said. "With the new players, we knew it was going to take some time for us to click as a group."

Since then, it has been Scherzer pitching seven scoreless innings with a broken nose and black eye. Or Turner returning to the lineup with an index finger on his throwing hand that he still can't make into a fist. Or Corbin pitching seven one-run innings and ignoring a 76-minute mid-start rain delay this week when he felt horribly distraught the day after the death of his close friend Tyler Skaggs of the Los Angeles Angels.

The schedule gets harder after the all-star break. Streaks like 26-10 eventually turn into normal seasons with long stretches of .500 until you catch fire again.

The dancing may be less frequent then. But whatever you do, don't let it stop.

The 12 best moments from the Nationals' 162-game thrill ride

By Scott Allen

Roller coaster. Sure, that's one way to sum up a Washington Nationals season that veered from near-lost cause in May to the National League wild-card game. Along the way, there were broken records, medical miracles and so much dancing. Here are the 12 best moments of the Nationals' 2019 regular season, in chronological order.

Kurt Suzuki got Gatorade showers after his three-run, walk-off home run against the Mets on Sept. 3 capped the biggest comeback in Nationals history. (John McDonnell/The Washington Post)

Anthony Rendon smacked a sixth-inning grand slam July 29, perhaps his biggest hit of the season. (Katherine Frey/The Washington Post)

April 2: Max Scherzer strikes out Bryce Harper

Harper's first of roughly 250 games at Nationals Park in a Phillies uniform over the next 13 years couldn't have gone much worse for the Nats, who watched Trea Turner suffer a broken index finger on a bunt attempt in the first inning and Philadelphia cruise to an 8-2 win on a dreary night.

Harper finished with three hits and a homer to help the Phillies improve to 4-0, but the night wasn't a total loss for the home crowd. Harper's pregame tribute video on the center field scoreboard was accompanied by sustained, cathartic boos. The jeers for the Liberty Bell lover were even louder when Harper came to the plate for the first time and struck out against Scherzer.

"The crowd was really into it, more so than I thought it would be," said Scherzer, who struck out Harper again in his second at-bat to set off another mini-celebration.

April 9: Victor Robles sparks comeback win

One week after Harper's return to D.C., the Nationals were down to their final strike at Citizens Bank Park after having trimmed a 6-1 deficit to 6-5. With Phillies fans on their feet and one holding a "WE GOT BRYCE, THANKS DC!!" sign, Victor Robles cranked a solo home run off Edubray Ramos to tie the score.

The Nationals added four runs in the 10th inning, with three of them coming on a moonshot home run by Juan Soto that hooked just inside the right field foul pole. The 20-year-old became the youngest player to hit a three-run homer in extra innings since Willie Mays in 1951.

"I think that's the hardest ball I've ever seen hit," Nationals Manager Dave Martinez said of Soto's blast.

May 11: Welcome to the Nats, Gerardo Parra

Parra had been with the Nationals for all of three days when he delivered the biggest hit of the team's season to date. With two outs in the eighth inning, the bases loaded and Washington trailing the Dodgers 2-1, the San Francisco Giants castoff launched Dylan Floro's pitch into the right-center field bleachers for a grand slam.

"Ah, we needed this," said Scherzer, who allowed two runs in seven innings. "That was a heck of an inning for us."

Max Scherzer, left, and Gerardo Parra celebrate after the Nationals clinched a playoff spot. (John McDonnell/The Washington Post)

The Nationals improved to 16-23 with the win. It was a sign of things to come from Parra.

June 9: Nats go back-to-back-to-back-to-back
The Nationals set a franchise record for home runs this season, including four in a span of seven pitches against a former Washington reliever. With the Nats and San Diego Padres tied at 1 in the eighth inning at Petco Park, Howie Kendrick, Turner, Adam Eaton and Anthony Rendon homered in consecutive at-bats off Craig Stammen.

The barrage, which took all of four minutes, marked the ninth time in major league history that a team had hit back-to-back-to-back-to-back home runs. The Nationals, who previously accomplished the feat July 27, 2017, against the Milwaukee Brewers, became the first team to do it twice.

"I liked the first one, for sure; that put us ahead," Martinez said. "And then it was wow . . . wow . . . and wow."

June 19: Scherzer pitches with a black eye
One day after he suffered a broken nose and a gnarly black eye on a bunt attempt gone wrong during batting practice, Scherzer struck out 10 Phillies over seven scoreless in a 2-0 Nationals win.

"This is just going to be part of what you got to do. You take the ball every fifth time," Scherzer said after the game, adding that he never considered skipping his turn in the rotation.

July 2: Patrick Corbin honors his late friend
Corbin took the mound with a heavy heart one day after Los Angeles Angels pitcher Tyler Skaggs, his friend and former teammate, died of an accidental drug overdose. Instead of his usual No. 46, Corbin wore Skaggs's No. 45 and drew those digits in the dirt on the back side of the mound at Nationals Park. Then he overcame a shaky first inning to limit the Miami Marlins to one run over seven innings in a 3-2 win.

"He's just all I'm thinking about," Corbin said after the game. ". . . When you have a loss, you want to keep things as normal as you can and just try to go out there and do what you have to do."

The "Baby Shark" movement started when Gerardo Parra switched his walk-up music June 19, spread when an animated graphic appeared July 23 and kept growing as the Nationals kept winning. (Toni L. Sandys/The Washington Post)

July 18: Stephen Strasburg dances

Strasburg had a dominant season, with a 3.32 ERA and a career-high 251 strikeouts while eclipsing 200 innings for the first time since 2014. But his most memorable game of the year had more to do with what he did with his bat.

In the first game of a pivotal midseason series at Atlanta, Strasburg allowed three runs and eight hits over five-plus innings. That was plenty good enough to earn his 12th win, thanks to his 3-for-3 night at the plate, which included a three-run homer and a career-high five RBI.

It wasn't until he reached the top step of the dugout after his home run that Strasburg realized he would have to dance for his teammates, as became custom for the Nationals. "To be honest, it was pretty nerve-racking," he said. "I didn't really have anything. I'm not a big dancer to begin with."

July 23: "Baby Shark" catches on

Not so much a moment as a movement, the Nationals' "Baby Shark" phenomenon originated June 19, when Parra, who was hitless in 22 straight at-bats, decided to change his walk-up song to the catchy children's tune.

"My girl loves that song," Parra said of his 2-year-old daughter, Aaliyah. ". . . She sings it a lot."

Parra went 2 for 4 with a home run and two RBI that day, and he hasn't changed his walk-up song since.

When Parra came to bat as a pinch hitter in the seventh inning with the bases loaded and looking to extend Washington's 5-0 lead against the Colorado Rockies on July 23, the Nationals debuted an animated graphic of Parra clapping along to the song on the center field scoreboard. Thousands of fans in the crowd of 22,612 stood and chomped as one before Parra cleared the bases with a single. Braves first baseman Freddie Freeman didn't know what to make of the singalong when Atlanta came to town a week later.

July 29: Rendon's grand slam sinks the Braves

During his MVP-caliber season, Rendon delivered a number of clutch hits, but perhaps none was bigger than his sixth-inning grand slam to break a 2-2 tie against the Braves at Nationals Park.

"I had to go back to my high school days. I did the 'Dougie' for a little bit; some of these people don't know about it," Rendon said of his ensuing dugout dance.

Washington went on to win, 6-3, to pull within 4½ games of Atlanta for the division lead. The Braves took the final two games of the series, and the Nationals would get no closer until the last day of the season, but for one night in late July, Rendon's heroics made it seem as if another NL East title was within reach.

Sept. 3: Kurt Suzuki caps incredible comeback against the Mets

The Nationals trailed the Mets 10-4 entering the bottom of the ninth inning. Seven runs later, with Scherzer watching Suzuki's walk-off home run on a TV in the bowels of Nationals Park, they had pulled off the biggest comeback in franchise history.

"If you walked out of this ballpark when the Mets scored five runs in the top of the ninth inning, YOU BLEW IT!" play-by-play man Charlie Slowes shouted on 106.7 the Fan. "A curly W's in the books!"

"I don't know, man," Ryan Zimmerman told Dan Kolko on the MASN postgame show. "I blacked out, and then we won."

The fan who caught Suzuki's home run ball joked that she blacked out, too.

The Mets had never lost a game they led by at least six runs in the ninth inning or later, and the Nationals became the first team since 1961 to allow five runs in the top of the ninth inning only to score more than five runs in the bottom of the ninth of a walk-off win.

Sept. 7: Aaron Barrett makes an emotional return

More than four years after his last appearance and more than three years after he broke the humerus in his right arm while throwing a fastball, Barrett pitched a scoreless inning of relief during a 5-4 loss at Atlanta. With several family members in the SunTrust Park stands, the 31-year-old walked one and struck out one without allowing a hit, and when he returned to the dugout, the tears flowed.

"After the outing was over, I'm just walking off, and all the emotions just hit me," Barrett said. "Just, you did it, man. You did it."

Sept. 24: Nats clinch after eliminating Phillies

With a 4-1 win in the first game of a split doubleheader, the Nationals officially eliminated Harper and the Phillies from playoff contention. A 6-5 win in the nightcap on the strength of Turner's grand slam, coupled with the Pirates' win over the Cubs, clinched a spot in the National League wild-card game.

The Nationals watched the final out of the Pirates-Cubs game, which was broadcast on the center field videoboard, before retreating to the clubhouse to celebrate with cheap beer and champagne.

"They want to keep playing. They don't quit," Martinez said during the booze-soaked dance party. "They keep telling me how much they want to play for me, and I told them it's not about me. It's about us. Let's play for us."

Honorable mentions: Turner walks off the Mets; Carter Kieboom homers in his first game; Robles makes a game-saving catch; Strasburg pitches an immaculate inning; Scherzer prematurely celebrates a walk-off that wasn't; Zimmerman collects career RBI No. 1,000; Turner becomes the 26th player to hit for the cycle twice; the Nats sweep the Cubs at Wrigley Field.

Trea Turner, racing to first June 5, hit
one of the back-to-back-to-back-to--back
home runs four days later.
(Jonathan Newton/The Washington Post)

With a broken face but an unbreakable will, Scherzer gives the Nats a defining moment

By Barry Svrluga

His normal sneer and snarl weren't enough, apparently, so Max Scherzer added something black, blue, disfigured, badass. Who's to say he didn't whisper to Bob Henley, the coach charged with throwing batting practice to the Washington Nationals' starting pitchers Tuesday, to fire one just a little up, just a little in? June baseball can get kind of slow, and the sub-.500 Nats could use a lift. What if he broke his nose — then pitched the next night anyway? Might be sort of fun.

Of the 4½ seasons in which Scherzer has graced us with his presence — 4½ seasons that include two no-hitters and a 20-strikeout game — Wednesday night may have been the most Max moment of them all, peak Scherzer. His face was broken and grotesque because of that fouled-off bunt attempt a day earlier. He could have gone right onto the set of "Game of Thrones" without reporting to makeup. How could he pitch? Are you kidding? How could he not pitch?

Whatever happens in this Nationals season — a season that took a step toward resurrection with a doubleheader sweep of the Philadelphia Phillies on Wednesday — we will have this gem, Scherzer at his competitive finest. His final line in the box score reads as Max at his healthiest: seven innings, four hits, no runs, two walks and 10 strikeouts in a 2-0 victory in the nightcap. Nothing out of the ordinary. See you again in five days.

This was different.

"I wanted to pitch. I didn't feel any p …" he said, stopping himself short. "Doesn't feel great. But I wanted to pitch."

He tried to downplay it: "On a scale of 1 to 10, the pain today was a zero," and, "Trust me, this looks a lot worse than it actually feels." And that's good because it looks terrible.

Don't think, though, that the clubhouse doesn't notice. It does. For a team that's fighting to stay afloat, that matters.

"It really is one of the most impressive things I've seen in a while," said second baseman Brian Dozier, who homered in both games. "He's probably the best pitcher of our generation, and you don't get that status unless you take the ball every fifth day — no matter if you're doing good, doing bad, you have a broken nose. You always want the ball."

It is, in baseball, the quality most admired. When Scherzer left the park Tuesday night, his face heavily bandaged, he was asked by various people how uncomfortable he was. Didn't matter, he responded. He would be pitching. He would be @!#&% pitching, thank you very much. When Dozier saw Scherzer preparing Wednesday afternoon, he ribbed him, "Ahh, you're going to pitch," as if he wasn't sure.

"He kind of gave me the go-to-hell look," Dozier said.

From even before his first-pitch slider for a strike to Phillies shortstop Jean Segura, it was obvious Scherzer wasn't treating this as any other start. His four-seam fastball this season, according to FanGraphs, had averaged 94.7 mph. Yet there he was with a 97-mph heater to Bryce Harper, the second hitter he faced. His first-inning fastballs averaged 96.5, more than a little hair on them. And there was more to come: three straight fastballs to absolutely destroy Brad Miller in the fourth — 96, 95 and 98, respectfully.

The capper, of course: a 98-mph seed past Miller for the first out of the seventh, then 97 mph to finish off Andrew Knapp for the second out of that frame and then an unfair slider down and away to put away pinch hitter J.T. Realmuto. With his 117th pitch done, he slapped his glove and twirled around. When he arrived at the top step of the dugout, hitting coach Kevin Long was the unfortunate soul who met him first. Max nearly took Long's arm off with a high-five.

"He hit my hand pretty hard," Manager Dave Martinez said. "He was fired up. The whole dugout was fired up."

For one of the few times all year. Maybe it took the ace to mess up his face to provide a pivot point for a team's season. How long till the Nats announce the date on the 2020 calendar for "Black-eye Max" bobblehead night?

Scherzer has to be disconcerting to face even as his regular self. His right eye is blue. His left eye is brown. He struts off the mound, kicks at the dirt, blows out his nose like a bull. It's a show. Every single time, it's a show.

But staring back at that visage Wednesday? His right

"Doesn's feel great," Max Scherzer said. "But I wanted to pitch." (John McDonnell/The Washington Post)

eye, the blue one, was dark and gloomy underneath. You want to say he looked as if he had been in a barroom brawl, but you know his response would be, "But you shoulda seen the other guy."

This makes no sense for anyone else. Given the point in the season, the strain it takes to get through 162 games, wouldn't wiser heads have said, "Take a day or three?" With rainouts Monday and Tuesday, the Nats had options. Patrick Corbin pitched in the opener. Erick Fedde was an option on regular rest in the nightcap. Scherzer could have pitched, say, Friday in the opener of a key series against division-leading Atlanta.

Except here's the thing: Scherzer knows — as everyone around the Nats knows — that there are no series that aren't key for this club right now.

"I knew I could post tonight," Scherzer said. So he posted.

The doubleheader sweep pulls the Nats to 35-38, the first time they have been within three games of .500 since April 29. For the Nationals to get all the way back into the race, they need Scherzer to will and inspire them.

Even before the whole seven-scoreless-with-a-busted-face thing, Scherzer was doing that. In his past six starts, he has a 0.88 ERA.

And now a real moment that could define a comeback. What was this like? This was like, say, Alex Ovechkin in January 2008, when the Montreal Canadiens busted his nose with a check, when he took a puck to the mouth and needed stitches — and scored four goals anyway. Hockey players, though, consider mangled faces a rite of passage. Scherzer is the rare baseball player who could wander into a hockey dressing room and fit right in.

Now, the big question: Will that attitude, that willingness not just to play but perform, help flip this season? I'm a believer that one game in 162 can mean more than another. That's what this felt like.

"That's what we're most focused on — just playing good baseball as a whole," Scherzer said. "When we can do that, we know we can compete with anybody in this league, and we can beat some teams."

They beat the Phillies on Wednesday night because Max Scherzer pitched when others would have sat. Scherzer doesn't need another signature moment, and he provided one anyway. If that doesn't serve as a turning point for this Nats season, nothing will.

Aren't playoff chases fun, Nats fans? Why are you hiding under your desk?

By Thomas Boswell

So we wanted to have a baseball team, did we? We thought it would be such a great idea, right? Especially the part about pennant races and tension and excitement throughout the whole month of September — all of it a stress test for October playoffs. What a fabulous roller-coaster ride, something that only baseball can provide day after day. Washington didn't have it for a third of a century. Now we do.

Are we having fun? Or are we ready to grill a burger on our frying-pan foreheads?

We were warned. We warned each other. But who listens, even to themselves? What the Washington Nationals and their followers are living right now — with their seven-game lead for a wild-card spot entering play Sept. 2 suddenly down to just 1½ games entering Thursday with 11 to play — is, if not the rule, very far from the exception in pennant races.

Odds, such as those 2½ weeks ago that said the Nats were better than 99 percent to be in the playoffs, are just elementary school arithmetic. In truth, September baseball is a game of streaks, shrieks and "OMG!"

Whatever you expect is constantly turned on its head. Are the Nats choking? Yes, certainly, to some degree. Their play in a 5-1 loss Wednesday in St. Louis had "pressure and how not to enjoy it" stamped on almost every inning.

But pennant races have many turning points, many chances to reboot the brain and spirit. Sometimes you just get lucky — if you can grab that good fortune and not turn it into another illustration that your rabbit's foot just got athlete's foot.

For example, the Nats now go to Miami for three games with the worst team in the NL: the Marlins, against whom they're 13-3. Meanwhile, the Chicago Cubs must play the tough St. Louis Cardinals seven times in the last 11 games, starting Thursday.

In just three days, things might and probably will look much different. But better? Or even worse? That's what's unusual about late-season baseball: Nothing happens for a long time, then everything happens all at once. To prepare our nervous systems for the Nats' last 11 games in 10 days starting Friday, this is what a playoff race feels like — on a no-good, very bad day.

In the second inning Wednesday afternoon in St. Louis, Nationals third base coach Bob Henley waved home Victor Robles from second base on a single by Max Scherzer. Robles was thrown out by 15 feet, ending an inning in which Trea Turner was due up next with the bases loaded.

For years, the brass has ordered "Sendley" to test outfielders' arms. The stats supposedly back this. Lord, does he oblige: The pile of dead ducks now seems as high as a D.C. monument. It sure fit the day's tone.

Later, Scherzer picked a Cardinal off second base, but Anthony Rendon froze and simply held the ball as two runners got back to their bases. In the seventh, a flyball that should have ended the inning with St. Louis ahead just 2-1 was lost in the sun by Juan Soto for a double.

Acting Nats manager Chip Hale let Scherzer try to get out of the inning, perhaps out of deference to his 11 strikeouts or his 97-mph fastball. It was a disaster. A squib scored a run. Still, Scherzer stayed. As if by cruel practical joke, Matt Wieters, a weak stick as a Nat, homered on Scherzer's 109th pitch. Ballgame: 5-1 loss.

Are the Nats, who have lost 10 of their past 16 games, falling apart under pressure? Will a spectacular 58-27 resurrection after a 19-31 start just be a footnote to a September choke, surpassing bitter Nats disappointments in division series? Could be. Heading that way.

But in a late race, almost every game contains more than one true perspective. Scherzer lost. But he was also Scherzer — finally. After 10 weeks as Hurt Max, Injured List Max, Reinjured Max, Back on the IL Max, Rehabilitating Max, Simulated Game Max, Pitch Limit Max, Training Wheels Max and Still Not Himself Max, Scherzer was finally a reasonable approximation of Hall of Fame hurler Mad Max.

If the Nats need him for two more regular season starts, he figures to be dominant again. If the Nats manage a wild-card spot before the last day of the season, he now looks like the proper choice to start. Before Wednesday, it was reasonable to wonder: If Max isn't Max, why bother with this whole October thing? It's not going anywhere.

On Monday, in a 4-2 loss, the Nats' other key back-from-IL pitcher, Sean Doolittle, showed progress but in an odd, worrisome way. He fanned a pair — but with a

The Nationals and their fans go wild as Trea Turner dives home for the game-winning run Aug. 30. (John McDonnell/The Washington Post)

change-up and slider. Not his fireballing style at all. He fired 93- to 95-mph fastballs at the letters but got foul balls, not swings and misses. His mechanics looked in sync, but that toe-tap delivery that Cubs Manager Joe Maddon claimed was illegal in the spring was back. That looks like a veteran pitcher grabbing for anything to get right.

If Doolittle can, like Scherzer, make one last jump up to "normal," he might complete a semi-decent bullpen. Remember, in this year of bullpen disasters, it's all relative. Since the All-Star Game, Daniel Hudson, Fernando Rodney, Wander Suero, Tanner Rainey and Hunter Strickland have a 3.62 ERA in 112 innings for the Nationals. Only Cleveland (3.56) has a lower bullpen ERA for the year. And 4.48 is now the major league average.

Of all the Nats' psychological weak points, the bullpen — with one save since Aug. 16 — is the one most likely to undermine the team's year-long resilience. But what if it started to be somewhat stable? Oh, forget I suggested it.

Also, the Nats probably will be helped if they can get Manager Dave Martinez back in the dugout. After

suffering chest pains Sunday, he underwent a cardiac catheterization to check his heart. He is apparently okay now. As soon as Martinez is cleared to fly, which may be as soon as Friday, General Manager Mike Rizzo said he can rejoin the team and manage. We may nag his bullpen managing, but let's not deny he has helped elevate team morale. His players might want to reverse roles and pick him up.

My wife, who likes sports but is not a "fan" of any of them, will not become a running character in this column, I promise. But she's on a hot streak — unlike the Nats. All year, she has listened to friends agonize about the Nats' bad start or awful bullpen or, now, September swoon. No amount of winning, even months of it, erases the next fear-fest.

"I hear sports is supposed to be 'the thrill of victory' and 'the agony of defeat,'" she said. "But all I see is the agony. Whatever happens, there's something to agonize about next. Why are people fans?"

Take a deep breath. In a dozen days, if anyone's left, maybe we will know.

2019 National League standings

EAST	W	L	PCT.	GB		CENTRAL	W	L	PCT.	GB		WEST	W	L	PCT.	GB
Atlanta Braves	97	65	.599	—		St. Louis Cardinals	91	71	.562	—		Los Angeles Dodgers	106	56	.654	—
Washington Nationals	93	69	.574	4		Milwaukee Brewers	89	73	.549	2		Arizona Diamondbacks	85	77	.525	21
New York Mets	86	76	.531	11		Chicago Cubs	84	78	.519	7		San Francisco Giants	77	85	.475	29
Philadelphia Phillies	81	81	.500	16		Cincinnati Reds	75	87	.463	16		Colorado Rockies	71	91	.438	35
Miami Marlins	57	105	.352	40		Pittsburgh Pirates	69	93	.426	22		San Diego Padres	70	92	.432	36

2019 American League standings

EAST	W	L	PCT.	GB		CENTRAL	W	L	PCT.	GB		WEST	W	L	PCT.	GB
New York Yankees	103	59	.636	—		Minnesota Twins	101	61	.623	—		Houston Astros	107	55	.660	—
Tampa Bay Rays	96	66	.593	7		Cleveland Indians	93	69	.574	8		Oakland Athletics	97	65	.599	10
Boston Red Sox	84	78	.519	19		Chicago White Sox	72	89	.447	28½		Texas Rangers	78	84	.481	29
Toronto Blue Jays	67	95	.414	36		Kansas City Royals	59	103	.364	42		Los Angeles Angels	72	90	.444	35
Baltimore Orioles	54	108	.333	49		Detroit Tigers	47	114	.292	53½		Seattle Mariners	68	94	.420	39

NL wild-card game: Washington def. Milwaukee. NLDS: Washington 3, Los Angeles 2; St. Louis 3, Atlanta 2. NLCS: Washington 4, St. Louis 0.
AL wild-card game: Tampa def. Oakland. ALDS: Houston 3, Tampa Bay 2; New York 3, Minnesota 0. ALCS: Houston 4, New York 2.
World Series: Washington def. Houston

Franchise history as Washington Nationals

	W	L	PCT.	FINISH	GB	R	RA	ATTENDANCE	TOP PLAYER (WAR)	MANAGERS
2019	93	69	.574	2nd	4	873	724	2,259,781	Strasburg (6.5)	Martinez
2018	82	80	.506	2nd	8	771	682	2,529,604	Scherzer (9.5)	Martinez
2017	97	65	.599	1st	—	819	672	2,524,980	Scherzer (7.5)	Baker
2016	95	67	.586	1st	—	763	612	2,481,938	Scherzer (6.5)	Baker
2015	83	79	.512	2nd	7	703	635	2,619,843	Harper (10.0)	Williams
2014	96	66	.593	1st	—	686	555	2,579,389	Rendon (6.6)	Williams
2013	86	76	.531	2nd	10	656	626	2,652,422	Werth (4.7)	Johnson
2012	98	64	.605	1st	—	731	594	2,370,794	Zimmermann (5.5)	Johnson
2011	80	81	.497	3rd	21½	624	643	1,940,478	Morse (3.4)	Riggleman, McLaren, Johnson
2010	69	93	.426	5th	28	655	742	1,828,066	Zimmerman (6.2)	Riggleman
2009	59	103	.364	5th	34	710	874	1,817,226	Zimmerman (7.3)	Acta, Riggleman
2008	59	102	.366	5th	32½	641	825	2,320,400	Guzman (4.6)	Acta
2007	73	89	.451	4th	16	673	783	1,943,812	Zimmerman (4.7)	Acta
2006	71	91	.438	5th	26	746	872	2,153,056	Soriano (6.1)	Robinson
2005	81	81	.500	5th	9	639	673	2,731,993	Patterson (4.5)	Robinson

Playoffs before 2019: Lost LDS (3-2) in 2012. Lost LDS (3-1) in 2014. Lost LDS (3-2) in 2016. Lost LDS (3-2) in 2017.

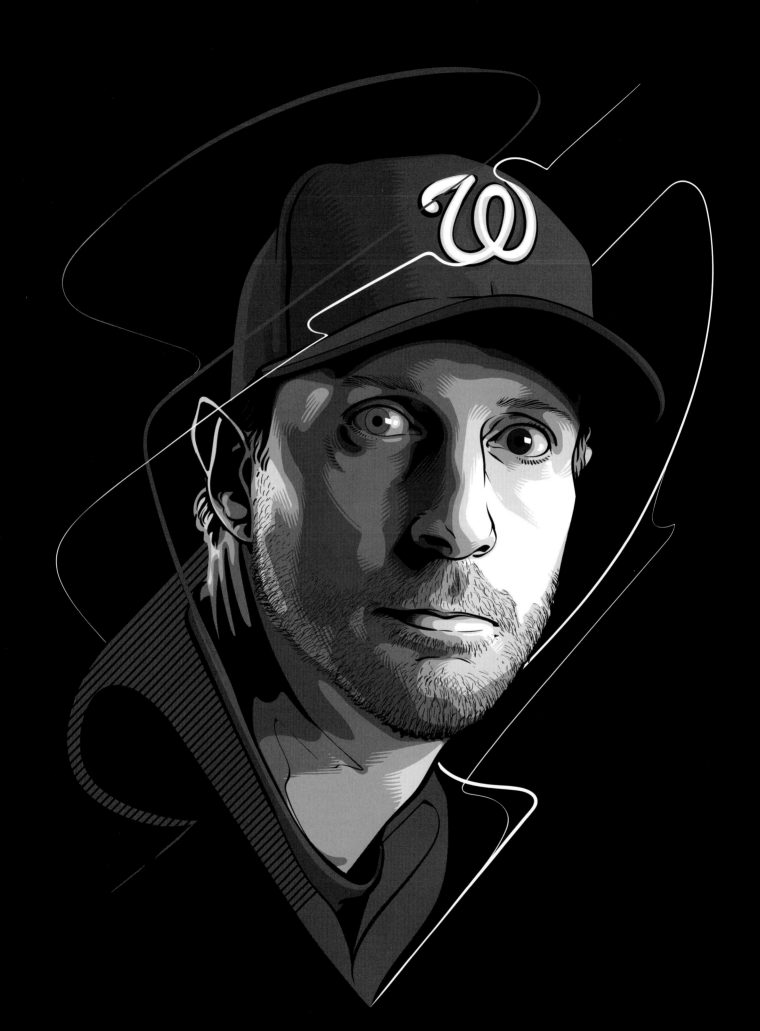

Washington Nationals regular season results (first half)

#	DATE	OPP	W/L	R	RA	INN	RK	GB	TIME	ATT
1	March 28	NYM	L	0	2		3	1	2:44	42,263
2	March 30	NYM	L	8	11		4	2	3:50	33,765
3	March 31	NYM	W*	6	5		4	2	3:15	23,430
4	April 2	PHI	L	2	8		3	3	3:30	35,920
5	April 3	PHI	W*	9	8		3	2.5	3:53	23,050
6	April 4	@NYM	W	4	0		3	1.5	3:19	44,424
7	April 6	@NYM	L	5	6		4	2.5	3:13	35,156
8	April 7	@NYM	W	12	9		4	2	3:42	40,681
9	April 8	@PHI	L	3	4		4	3	2:32	28,212
10	April 9	@PHI	W	10	6	10	4	2	3:51	38,073
11	April 10	@PHI	W	15	1		4	1	3:35	30,805
12	April 12	PIT	L	3	6	10	4	2.5	3:28	27,084
13	April 13	PIT	W	3	2		4	1.5	2:22	32,103
14	April 14	PIT	L	3	4		4	2	2:47	22,347
15	April 16	SFG	L	3	7		4	2.5	3:16	22,334
16	April 17	SFG	W	9	6		4	2.5	3:07	22,611
17	April 18	SFG	W	4	2		3	1.5	2:52	26,085
18	April 19	@MIA	L	2	3		3	1.5	2:52	8,199
19	April 20	@MIA	L	3	9		4	2.5	3:12	9,910
20	April 21	@MIA	W	5	0		4	1.5	2:45	7,412
21	April 22	@COL	L	5	7		4	1.5	3:00	20,517
22	April 23	@COL	W	6	3		3	1.5	3:14	24,456
23	April 24	@COL	L	5	9		4	1.5	2:48	33,135
24	April 26	SDP	L	3	4		4	2	3:02	27,193
25	April 27	SDP	L	3	8	10	4	3	3:45	35,422
26	April 28	SDP	W*	7	6	11	4	3	4:03	30,186
27	April 29	STL	L	3	6		4	3.5	3:05	17,890
28	April 30	STL	L	2	3		4	3.5	3:09	19,753
29	May 1	STL	L	1	5		4	4.5	3:02	22,157
30	May 2	STL	W	2	1		4	4	3:00	24,338
31	May 3	@PHI	L	2	4		4	5	2:42	33,125
32	May 4	@PHI	W	10	8		4	4	3:45	43,319
33	May 5	@PHI	L	1	7		4	5	3:03	40,497
34	May 6	@MIL	L	3	5		4	5	3:33	29,299
35	May 7	@MIL	L	0	6		4	6	3:00	31,023
36	May 8	@MIL	L	3	7		4	7	3:24	30,333
37	May 9	@LAD	W	6	0		4	6.5	3:11	42,851
38	May 10	@LAD	L	0	5		4	6.5	2:58	43,533
39	May 11	@LAD	W	5	2		4	6.5	2:58	53,647
40	May 12	@LAD	L	0	6		4	7.5	2:46	45,667
41	May 14	NYM	L	2	6		4	8	2:38	23,315
42	May 15	NYM	W	5	1		4	7	2:28	29,673
43	May 16	NYM	W	7	6		4	6	3:16	28,807
44	May 17	CHC	L	6	14		4	7	4:09	33,296
45	May 18	CHC	W	5	2		4	7	2:56	37,582
46	May 19	CHC	L	5	6		4	8	3:15	23,244
47	May 20	@NYM	L	3	5		4	9	3:12	22,335
48	May 21	@NYM	L*	5	6		4	9	3:05	24,631
49	May 22	@NYM	L	1	6		4	9	2:59	27,188
50	May 23	@NYM	L	4	6		4	10	2:53	29,962
51	May 24	MIA	W	12	10		4	10	3:59	29,173
52	May 25	MIA	W	5	0		4	10	2:25	33,163
53	May 26	MIA	W	9	6		4	9	3:06	26,365
54	May 27	MIA	L	2	3		4	9.5	3:00	21,048
55	May 28	@ATL	W	5	4		4	9.5	3:21	27,573
56	May 29	@ATL	W	14	4		4	9.5	3:11	37,726
57	May 31	@CIN	L	3	9		4	9	2:49	24,358
58	June 1	@CIN	W	5	2		4	8	2:59	27,748
59	June 2	@CIN	W	4	1		4	7	3:07	22,801
60	June 4	CHW	W	9	5		4	6.5	3:33	32,513
61	June 5	CHW	W*	6	4		4	6.5	3:07	28,910
62	June 6	@SDP	L	4	5		4	7	3:07	19,908
63	June 7	@SDP	L*	4	5		4	8	2:46	21,645
64	June 8	@SDP	W	4	1		4	8	2:39	30,319
65	June 9	@SDP	W	5	2		4	7	2:56	30,518
66	June 10	@CHW	W	12	1		4	6	3:06	16,305
67	June 11	@CHW	L	5	7		4	7	3:19	16,790
68	June 13	ARI	L	0	5		4	8.5	2:15	24,909
69	June 14	ARI	W	7	3		4	8.5	2:57	29,853
70	June 15	ARI	L	3	10		4	8.5	3:30	38,044
71	June 16	ARI	W	15	5		4	8.5	3:14	29,032
72	June 19 (1)	PHI	W	6	2		3	8	2:46	17,961
73	June 19 (2)	PHI	W	2	0		3	8	3:05	24,220
74	June 20	PHI	W	7	4		3	7.5	3:05	31,329
75	June 21	ATL	W	4	3		3	6.5	3:01	34,212
76	June 22	ATL	L	9	13		3	7.5	3:42	37,492
77	June 23	ATL	L	3	4	10	3	8.5	3:09	34,256
78	June 25	@MIA	W	6	1		3	8	2:27	7,327
79	June 26	@MIA	W	7	5		3	8	3:19	6,276
80	June 27	@MIA	W	8	5		3	7	2:51	7,751
81	June 28	@DET	W	3	1		3	7	3:04	20,877

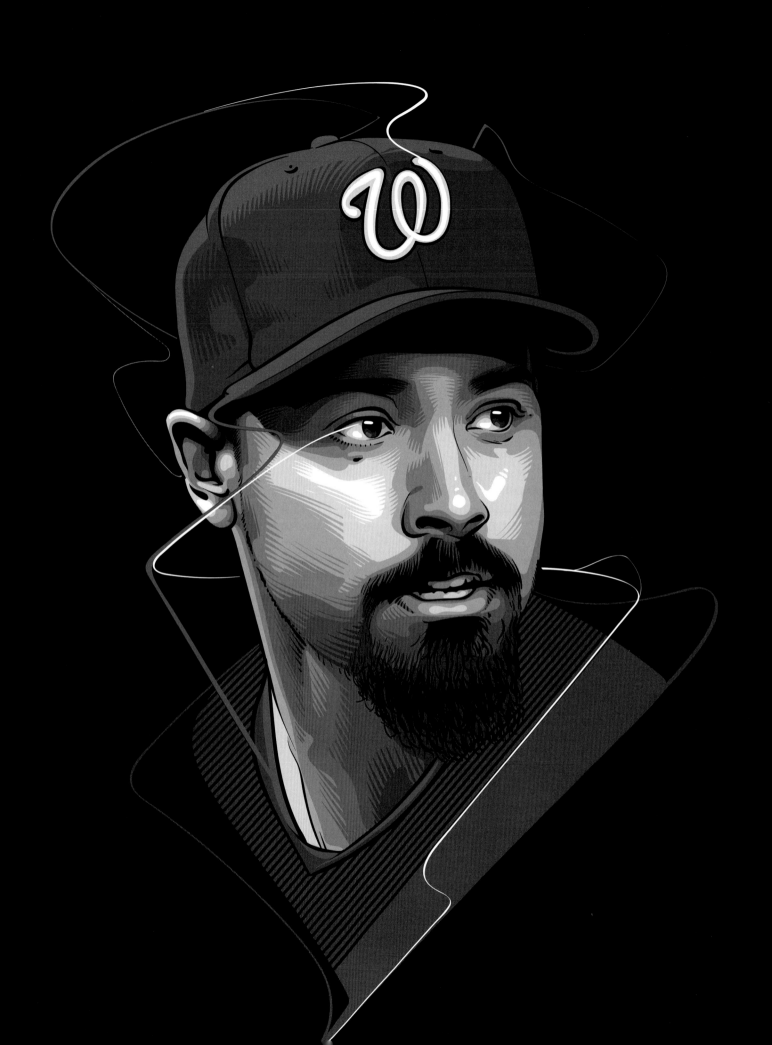

Washington Nationals regular season results (second half)

	DATE	OPP	W/L	R	RA	INN	RK	GB	TIME	ATT
82	June 29	@DET	L	5	7		3	8	3:13	27,716
83	June 30	@DET	W	2	1		3	7	2:53	21,052
84	July 2	MIA	W*	3	2		3	6	3:01	21,361
85	July 3	MIA	W	3	1		3	6	3:07	25,483
86	July 4	MIA	W	5	2		2	6	3:17	27,350
87	July 5	KCR	L	4	7	11	3	7	4:40	25,213
88	July 6	KCR	W	6	0		2	6	2:44	27,863
89	July 7	KCR	W	5	2		2	6	2:37	21,873
90	July 12	@PHI	W	4	0		2	6	3:15	42,318
91	July 13	@PHI	W	4	3		2	6	3:43	43,732
92	July 14	@PHI	L*	3	4		2	7	2:54	43,075
93	July 16	@BAL	W	8	1		2	6.5	3:10	23,362
94	July 17	@BAL	L	2	9		2	6.5	2:51	20,786
95	July 18	@ATL	W	13	4		2	5.5	3:44	39,363
96	July 19	@ATL	L*	3	4		2	6.5	3:30	39,344
97	July 20	@ATL	W	5	3		2	5.5	3:14	42,467
98	July 21	@ATL	L	1	7		2	6.5	3:02	31,848
99	July 23	COL	W	11	1		2	5.5	3:37	22,612
100	July 24 (1)	COL	W	3	2		2	4	3:03	14,628
101	July 24 (2)	COL	W	2	0		2	4	3:07	23,843
102	July 25	COL	L	7	8		2	4.5	3:46	26,831
103	July 26	LAD	L	2	4		2	5.5	3:20	37,491
104	July 27	LAD	L	3	9		2	6.5	3:06	39,616
105	July 28	LAD	W	11	4		2	5.5	3:09	32,425
106	July 29	ATL	W	6	3		2	4.5	3:23	24,292
107	July 30	ATL	L	8	11		2	5.5	3:47	26,566
108	July 31	ATL	L	4	5	10	2	6.5	3:14	31,576
109	Aug. 2	@ARI	W	3	0		2	6	2:43	24,298
110	Aug. 3	@ARI	L	7	18		2	7	3:46	33,966
111	Aug. 4	@ARI	L	5	7		2	7	3:07	22,976
112	Aug. 5	@SFG	W	4	0		2	6	3:12	32,366
113	Aug. 6	@SFG	W	5	3		2	6	2:45	31,628
114	Aug. 7	@SFG	W	4	1		2	6	2:59	30,958
115	Aug. 9	@NYM	L*	6	7		2	6.5	3:20	39,602
116	Aug. 10	@NYM	L	3	4		2	6.5	2:34	43,875
117	Aug. 11	@NYM	W	7	4		2	6.5	3:35	41,000
118	Aug. 12	CIN	W	7	6		2	6	3:11	22,394
119	Aug. 13	CIN	W	3	1		2	6	2:38	30,130
120	Aug. 14	CIN	W	17	7		2	6	3:38	23,596
121	Aug. 16	MIL	W	2	1		2	4.5	3:00	30,091
122	Aug. 17	MIL	L	14	15	14	2	5.5	5:40	36,953
123	Aug. 18	MIL	W	16	8		2	5.5	3:24	30,571
124	Aug. 19	@PIT	W	13	0		2	5	3:16	11,284
125	Aug. 20	@PIT	L	1	4		2	6	3:00	10,449
126	Aug. 21	@PIT	W	11	1		2	6	2:54	10,577
127	Aug. 22	@PIT	W	7	1		2	6	3:19	10,587
128	Aug. 23	@CHC	W	9	3		2	6	3:10	39,889
129	Aug. 24	@CHC	W	7	2		2	6	3:56	40,658
130	Aug. 25	@CHC	W	7	5	11	2	6	4:35	40,518
131	Aug. 27	BAL	L	0	2		2	5.5	2:52	24,946
132	Aug. 28	BAL	W	8	4		2	5.5	3:12	25,174
133	Aug. 30	MIA	W*	7	6		2	5.5	3:35	26,201
134	Aug. 31	MIA	W	7	0		2	5.5	2:31	27,539
135	Sept. 1	MIA	W	9	3		2	5.5	2:46	29,345
136	Sept. 2	NYM	L	3	7		2	6.5	3:08	25,329
137	Sept. 3	NYM	W*	11	10		2	6.5	3:17	20,759
138	Sept. 4	NYM	L	4	8		2	7	3:24	20,237
139	Sept. 5	@ATL	L	2	4		2	8	2:57	28,831
140	Sept. 6	@ATL	L	3	4		2	9	3:20	37,181
141	Sept. 7	@ATL	L	4	5		2	10	3:29	40,467
142	Sept. 8	@ATL	W	9	4		2	9	3:16	31,789
143	Sept. 10	@MIN	L	0	5		2	9.5	2:32	24,813
144	Sept. 11	@MIN	W	6	2		2	9.5	3:12	20,062
145	Sept. 12	@MIN	W	12	6		2	8.5	3:45	19,167
146	Sept. 13	ATL	L	0	5		2	9.5	3:16	39,730
147	Sept. 14	ATL	L	1	10		2	10.5	3:29	39,664
148	Sept. 15	ATL	W	7	0		2	9.5	3:03	29,350
149	Sept. 16	@STL	L	2	4		2	10	3:04	42,812
150	Sept. 17	@STL	W	6	2		2	9	3:21	44,061
151	Sept. 18	@STL	L	1	5		2	9	2:55	37,669
152	Sept. 20	@MIA	W	6	4		2	9.5	3:13	12,775
153	Sept. 21	@MIA	W	10	4	10	2	9.5	4:20	18,085
154	Sept. 22	@MIA	L	3	5		2	9.5	3:13	19,709
155	Sept. 23	PHI	W	7	2		2	9	3:19	19,788
156	Sept. 24 (1)	PHI	W	4	1		2	7.5	3:07	23,442
157	Sept. 24 (2)	PHI	W	6	5		2	7.5	3:06	22,214
158	Sept. 25	PHI	W	5	2		2	7.5	2:45	22,091
159	Sept. 26	PHI	W	6	3		2	7	3:26	22,253
160	Sept. 27	CLE	W	8	2		2	6	2:44	27,434
161	Sept. 28	CLE	W	10	7		2	5	3:10	38,435
162	Sept. 29	CLE	W	8	2		2	4	2:50	36,764

*walk-off

Washington Nationals regular season batting

		G	AB	R	H	2B	3B	HR	RBI	SB	CS	BB	SO	BA	OBP	SLG	OPS
C	Yan Gomes	97	314	36	70	16	0	12	43	2	0	38	84	.223	.316	.389	.704
1B	Matt Adams*	111	310	42	70	14	0	20	56	0	0	20	115	.226	.276	.465	.741
2B	Brian Dozier	135	416	54	99	20	0	20	50	3	4	61	105	.238	.340	.430	.771
SS	Trea Turner	122	521	96	155	37	5	19	57	35	5	43	113	.298	.353	.497	.850
3B	Anthony Rendon	146	545	117	174	44	3	34	126	5	1	80	86	.319	.412	.598	1.010
LF	Juan Soto*	150	542	110	153	32	5	34	110	12	1	108	132	.282	.401	.548	.949
CF	Victor Robles	155	546	86	139	33	3	17	65	28	9	35	140	.255	.326	.419	.745
RF	Adam Eaton*	151	566	103	158	25	7	15	49	15	3	65	106	.279	.365	.428	.792
IF	Howie Kendrick	121	334	61	115	23	1	17	62	2	1	27	49	.344	.395	.572	.966
C	Kurt Suzuki	85	280	37	74	11	0	17	63	0	1	20	36	.264	.324	.486	.809
UT	Gerardo Parra*	89	188	30	47	11	1	8	42	6	2	11	41	.250	.300	.447	.747
1B	Ryan Zimmerman	52	171	20	44	9	0	6	27	0	0	17	39	.257	.321	.415	.736
2B	Asdrúbal Cabrera**	38	124	24	40	10	1	6	40	0	0	19	18	.323	.404	.565	.969
SS	Wilmer Difo**	43	131	15	33	2	0	2	8	0	1	12	29	.252	.315	.313	.628
CF	Michael A. Taylor	53	88	10	22	7	0	1	3	6	0	7	34	.250	.305	.364	.669
SS	Carter Kieboom	11	39	4	5	0	0	2	2	0	0	4	16	.128	.209	.282	.491
LF	Andrew Stevenson*	30	30	4	11	1	1	0	0	0	1	6	11	.367	.486	.467	.953
UT	Adrián Sanchez	28	31	3	7	0	0	0	1	0	0	1	10	.226	.250	.226	.476
IF	Jake Noll	8	12	1	2	1	0	0	2	0	0	1	4	.167	.231	.250	.481
C	Raudy Read	6	11	0	1	0	0	0	0	0	0	0	5	.091	.091	.091	.182
P	Stephen Strasburg	33	72	4	12	1	0	1	10	0	0	3	25	.167	.200	.222	.422
P	Patrick Corbin*	31	65	3	6	1	0	0	4	0	0	3	27	.092	.132	.108	.240
P	Max Scherzer	28	55	6	10	0	0	0	2	2	0	0	27	.182	.182	.182	.364
P	Anibál Sánchez	27	52	1	6	0	0	0	1	0	0	0	24	.115	.115	.115	.231
P	Joe Ross	28	19	1	2	0	0	0	0	0	0	1	10	.105	.150	.105	.255
P	Erick Fedde	20	15	1	2	0	0	0	0	0	0	0	6	.133	.133	.133	.267
	Team totals	162	5,512	873	1,460	298	27	231	824	116	29	584	1,308	.265	.342	.454	.796
	NL rank		9	2	3	6	5	6		1	9	4	2	2	1	3	2

Minimum 10 at-bats

*Bats left
**Bats both

Washington Nationals regular season pitching

		W	L	ERA	G	GS	GF	CG	SV	IP	H	R	ER	HR	BB	SO	WHIP
RH	Stephen Strasburg	18	6	3.32	33	33	0	0	0	209	161	79	77	24	56	251	1.038
LH	Patrick Corbin	14	7	3.25	33	33	0	1	0	202	169	81	73	24	70	238	1.183
RH	Max Scherzer	11	7	2.92	27	27	0	0	0	172⅓	144	59	56	18	33	243	1.027
RH	Aníbal Sánchez	11	8	3.85	30	30	0	0	0	166	153	77	71	22	58	134	1.271
RH	Erick Fedde	4	2	4.50	21	12	3	0	0	78	81	39	39	11	33	41	1.462
LH	Sean Doolittle	6	5	4.05	63	0	55	0	29	60	63	27	27	11	15	66	1.300
RH	Wander Suero	6	9	4.54	78	0	10	0	1	71⅓	64	36	36	5	26	81	1.262
RH	Javy Guerra	3	1	4.86	40	0	15	0	1	53⅔	55	30	29	9	12	42	1.248
RH	Tanner Rainey	2	3	3.91	52	0	7	0	0	48⅓	32	22	21	6	38	74	1.448
LH	Matt Grace	1	2	6.36	51	1	12	0	0	46⅔	61	34	33	11	10	35	1.521
RH	Joe Ross	4	4	5.48	27	9	3	0	0	64	74	41	39	7	33	57	1.672
RH	Austin Voth	2	1	3.30	9	8	0	0	0	43⅔	33	16	16	5	13	44	1.053
RH	Jeremy Hellickson	2	3	6.23	9	8	1	0	0	39	47	31	27	9	20	30	1.718
RH	Fernando Rodney	0	3	4.05	38	0	8	0	2	33⅓	29	16	15	3	16	35	1.350
RH	Kyle Barraclough	1	2	6.66	33	0	6	0	0	25⅔	33	21	19	8	12	30	1.753
RH	Daniel Hudson	3	0	1.44	24	0	14	0	6	25	18	7	4	3	4	23	0.880
LH	Tony Sipp	1	2	4.71	36	0	7	0	0	21	19	12	11	1	9	18	1.333
RH	Hunter Strickland	2	0	5.14	24	0	1	0	0	21	20	12	12	5	8	15	1.333
RH	Kyle McGowin	0	0	10.13	7	1	4	0	1	16	22	19	18	7	4	18	1.625
RH	Justin Miller	1	0	4.02	17	0	5	0	0	15⅔	16	8	7	5	4	11	1.277
RH	Trevor Rosenthal	0	1	22.74	12	0	5	0	0	6⅓	8	16	16	0	15	5	3.632
RH	Michael Blazek	0	0	7.20	4	0	3	0	0	5	6	4	4	1	5	0	2.200
LH	Dan Jennings	1	2	13.50	8	0	0	0	0	4⅔	8	8	7	1	7	9	3.214
LH	Jonny Venters	0	1	5.40	3	0	1	0	0	3⅓	3	3	2	0	2	5	1.500
LH	Roenis Elías	0	0	9.00	4	0	0	0	0	3	5	4	3	2	1	2	2.000
RH	Aaron Barrett	0	0	15.43	3	0	0	0	0	2⅓	5	4	4	1	4	1	3.857
RH	Brian Dozier	0	0	18.00	1	0	1	0	0	1	2	2	2	1	0	0	2.000
RH	Austin Adams	0	0	9.00	1	0	0	0	0	1	0	1	1	0	2	2	2.000
RH	James Bourque	0	0	54.00	1	0	0	0	0	⅔	3	4	4	0	2	0	7.500
RH	Austen Williams	0	0	162.00	2	0	0	0	0	⅓	5	6	6	2	1	1	18.000
LH	Gerardo Parra	0	0	inf	1	0	0	0	0	0	1	5	5	0	4	0	
	Team totals	93	69	4.27	162	162	161	1	40	1,439⅓	1,340	724	683	202	517	1,511	1.29
	NL rank	3	13	8				5	9	13	4	5	6	4	5	4	

Shutouts: Corbin 1

Sean Doolittle (Cristiano Siqueira illustration)

Washington Nationals postseason batting

	G	AB	R	H	2B	3B	HR	RBI	BB	SO	SB	CS	AVG	OBP	SLG	OPS
Michael A. Taylor	8	21	4	7	0	0	2	2	1	7	0	0	.333	.391	.619	1.010
Matt Adams	4	3	1	1	0	0	0	0	1	1	0	0	.333	.500	.333	.833
Anthony Rendon	17	61	11	20	7	0	3	15	11	10	0	0	.328	.413	.590	1.003
Howie Kendrick	17	63	8	18	4	0	2	12	4	11	0	0	.286	.328	.444	.773
Juan Soto	17	65	12	18	3	0	5	14	9	21	1	0	.277	.373	.554	.927
Ryan Zimmerman	16	55	5	14	3	0	2	7	5	17	0	0	.255	.317	.418	.735
Adam Eaton	17	61	11	15	2	1	2	10	10	9	1	0	.246	.361	.410	.771
Yan Gomes	11	29	3	7	2	0	0	3	2	9	0	0	.241	.290	.310	.601
Trea Turner	17	73	10	17	4	0	1	3	6	15	1	0	.233	.291	.329	.620
Asdrúbal Cabrera	12	30	1	7	1	0	0	5	1	10	0	0	.233	.250	.267	.517
Victor Robles	12	41	8	9	1	1	1	3	2	15	1	0	.220	.273	.366	.639
Gerardo Parra	7	6	1	1	0	0	0	0	1	2	0	0	.167	.286	.167	.452
Kurt Suzuki	10	30	2	3	0	0	1	1	4	11	0	0	.100	.229	.200	.429
Brian Dozier	8	6	0	0	0	0	0	0	1	2	0	0	.000	.143	.000	.143

Washington Nationals postseason pitching

	W	L	ERA	G	GS	SV	SVO	IP	H	R	ER	HR	BB	SO	AVG	WHIP
Sean Doolittle	0	0	1.74	9	0	2	2	10⅓	6	2	2	1	1	8	.167	0.68
Stephen Strasburg	5	0	1.98	6	5	0	0	36⅓	30	9	8	4	4	47	.221	0.94
Max Scherzer	3	0	2.40	6	5	0	0	30	21	8	8	4	15	37	.193	1.20
Aníbal Sánchez	1	1	2.50	3	3	0	0	18	15	5	5	2	4	18	.221	1.06
Javy Guerra	0	0	3.00	2	0	0	0	3	6	1	1	1	0	1	.400	2.00
Daniel Hudson	1	0	3.72	9	0	4	4	9⅔	11	4	4	1	4	10	.275	1.55
Fernando Rodney	0	0	3.86	6	0	0	0	4⅔	4	2	2	1	9	5	.222	2.79
Wander Suero	0	0	4.50	4	0	0	0	2	2	1	1	1	0	2	.250	1.00
Joe Ross	0	1	5.14	2	1	0	0	7	6	4	4	2	2	1	.240	1.14
Patrick Corbin	2	3	5.79	8	3	0	1	23⅓	21	16	15	2	12	36	.233	1.41
Tanner Rainey	0	0	6.75	9	0	0	0	6⅔	3	5	5	1	5	6	.130	1.20
Hunter Strickland	0	0	18.00	2	0	0	0	2	4	4	4	3	1	3	.400	2.50

Victor Robles celebrates during the Nationals' six-run seventh inning in Game 2 of the World Series. (Toni L. Sandys/The Washington Post)